GW00367302

From

A Cornish Bishop's Garden

1   *Lis Escop in 1914, after it had been enlarged.*

From

A Cornish Bishop's Garden

Joseph Wellington Hunkin

Edited with an Introduction

by

Douglas Ellory Pett

First published in 2001 by
Alison Hodge
Bosulval, Newmill, Penzance, Cornwall TR20 8XA

This edition © Alison Hodge, 2001
© Douglas Ellory Pett 2001

The right of Douglas Ellory Pett to be identified as author
of this work has been asserted by him in accordance with
the Copyright, Designs and Patents Act 1988.

All rights reserved. Apart from any fair dealing for the
purpose of private study, research, criticism or review,
as permitted under the Copyright, Designs and Patents Act
1988, no part of this work may be photocopied, stored in
a retrieval system, published, performed in public, adapted,
broadcast, transmitted, recorded or reproduced in any
form or by any means, without the prior permission
in writing of the copyright owner. Enquiries should be
addressed to Alison Hodge.

ISBN 0 906720 30 3

British Library Cataloguing-in-Publication Data
A catalogue record for this book is available from the
British Library.

Designed and typeset by BDP –
Book Development and Production, Penzance, Cornwall

Printed and bound in the UK by TJ International Ltd.,
Padstow, Cornwall PL28 8RW

Contents

Illustrations

Foreword

The Rt Revd William Ind, Bishop of Truro

In October 2000, about 200 people came to a lecture and then to a memorial service held in Truro Cathedral, to remember Bishop Hunkin on the fiftieth anniversary of his death. The only Cornishman to be Bishop of Truro, he was, as his memorial in the Cathedral says, 'A man greatly beloved'.

As Bishop of Truro, I cannot help but be aware of my predecessors – indeed I say goodnight to them every night. Their portraits are prominent on the stairs and among them is Bishop Hunkin. His family says that the portrait is not a good likeness, but at least there is a flower in the vase next to him. The pity is that it is not a particularly Cornish flower like a camellia, rhododendron or azalea, but in fact is a rather ordinary viburnum. At least, though, the flower is a symbol and a reminder of the Bishop's 'hinterland'. As a Diocesan Bishop, he was busy with all the aspects of Cornish life, as his biographer makes clear, but still he found time to have a passionate interest in plants and the gardens of Cornwall and beyond.

We are all in Douglas Pett's debt for gathering together in this book the articles that Bishop Hunkin wrote in the church weekly *The Guardian*. The articles make clear the Bishop's passion for gardens and plants and his deep knowledge. They do more than this though – they reveal the Bishop's humanity and warmth. The style in which the articles are written is both learned and approachable, and tells us something of the Bishop as an amateur – that is, a person who is a lover of Cornwall and its gardens.

This book deserves to be read for its own sake, because the articles in it have a freshness in their descriptions which has not faded over the fifty and more years since they were written.

Of particular interest, perhaps, is the comprehensive list of plants given after the Bishop's death as a living memorial. There they are in parishes up and down the Diocese, listed fully. How

many of them are still there? Douglas Pett has not himself found
many of them. Perhaps one response to reading this book is to go
out and look in the churchyards of the Diocese. Perhaps, too, in the
year of the 125th anniversary of the Diocese of Truro, we can
begin to replace the plants that have been lost. That will be a real
sign that the memory of a good man has not been forgotten.

2   *Diocese of Truro, coat of arms.*

Introduction

It would be no exaggeration to claim that Bishop Hunkin in the middle of the last century was one of the leading Cornish horticultural writers, although since, unlike Edgar Thurston or Arnold-Forster, he wrote no book, but contributed his more serious articles to specialist journals, his gardening writings are little known to the public at large. The forty charming articles written in a more easy style, which *were* addressed to the ordinary reader, however, appeared in a church weekly – *The Guardian* – which ceased publication in 1951, so that it is rarely found in libraries and is now long forgotten.

This present book is intended to rescue them from the oblivion into which they have fallen by collecting all of the *Guardian* articles under one cover, as a lasting tribute to Bishop Hunkin, in commemoration of the fiftieth anniversary of his untimely death. The long series of articles in the same journal by Canon Ellacombe of Bitton, during the years 1890–1909 were later published in two volumes, and those of the perhaps more celebrated Gertrude Jekyll in 1896–7 form the substance of her familiar book *Wood and Garden* (1899). It seems, then, only right and proper that the Bishop's no less interesting and lasting essays should be similarly preserved for posterity.

Joseph Wellington Hunkin was born of Methodist parents at 16 The Parade, Truro, along the road to Malpas, on 25 September 1887. He began his education at Truro College (now Truro School), passing on to the Leys Methodist public school at Cambridge, and thence to Gonville and Caius College, where he achieved distinction in Mathematics. In 1913 he was ordained into the Church of England, receiving his title at St Andrew's, Plymouth, before becoming vice-principal at Wycliffe Hall, Oxford, being elected Fellow of his old college from 1913 to 1927. The First World War interrupted his academic career when he became a chaplain to the 29th Division, where he served with exceptional courage, resulting in the award of the MC and bar, and the receiving of an OBE on demobilisation. After the war he returned to Gonville and Caius as Dean and tutor. Although he had aspirations to continue teaching at the University, he accepted the challenge of pastoral work as Archdeacon of Coventry and rector of St Andrew's with Holy Trinity, Rugby. He received the degree of Doctor of Divinity in 1930, and was appointed Hulsean Preacher at Cambridge the following year.

There is nothing in this brief synopsis of Hunkin's life[1] to hint that he would later become a great horticultural writer; indeed there is little evidence of any opportunity for practical experience in gardening. If we are to discover the seeds of his later interest in plants, we must dig deeper into his early life. The Parade, Truro, faces the river, a short distance from the then recently laid out Boscawen Park, where he would have played as a boy, and on river trips in his father's boat have seen the great parks around Tregothnan and Trelissick. Above The Parade were the grounds of Tregolls House, and along the road out of Truro were Alverton House (then the Convent), Tremorvah, and Pencalenick, which he would have passed on his first outing as a local preacher at the little chapel by Tresillian Bridge. To be brought up in such a rich tapestry of gardens, and to walk through woodlands and lanes seeing the Cornish hedges bedecked in spring with primroses could not fail to make its impression upon his young mind. Many years later, in one of the *Guardian* articles, he quoted from Gertrude Jekyll's own reminiscences, words which he probably selected because they echoed his own experiences.

> It must have been at about seven years of age that I first learnt to know and love a primrose copse. Since then more than half a century has passed ... [yet] when I see and feel and hear all this, for a moment I am seven years old again and wandering in the fragrant wood hand-in-hand with the dear God who made it, and who made the child's mind to open wide and receive the enduring happiness of the gracious gift.

Bishop Hunkin's studies at Cambridge had touched on the natural sciences, and he relates in the lives of the early botanists, almost all clergymen or devout laymen, influences which may well have had parallels in his own life. The great naturalist John Ray, for example, convalescing from an early illness, he quoted as writing, 'First the rich array of spring-time meadows, then the shape, colour and structure of particular plants fascinated and absorbed me: botany became a passion.' The description of plants in the *Guardian* articles exhibits this same wonder at the minute details in flowers. He also recollected John Wesley's remark about another botanist, Stephen Hales – 'how well do philosophy and religion agree in a man of sound understanding'. In what was to be the Bishop's last article in *The Guardian* he returned once again to the Cambridge that he loved, to contrast the improvements made in the college gardens with what he had known there as a student. He thought that if this continued the sister University of Oxford 'will have to look to her laurels'. That may be so, but no impartial observer can deny that the idyllic setting and beauty of Cambridge surpasses that of industrial Oxford, and it was in this atmosphere that he spent his formative years.

Bishop Hunkin became well known in his theological works for seeking to reconcile religious beliefs with the findings of modern science. But there is no hint in his articles of the outdated 'evidences of religion' approach or sentimentality, which he abhorred. His articles are nevertheless instinct with a love of the God who created the beauty around him, which, as for John Ray 'fascinated and absorbed' him.

In 1935 Joseph Wellington Hunkin was offered the bishopric of Truro, to become the first and only Cornish bishop in modern times. He accepted, memorably expressing his feelings at his enthronement: 'I am come home. This is my call. I expect no other.'

Lis Escop

The Cornish *Lis Escop* means 'Bishop's Palace', yet this was no mansion, but simply the converted parsonage of St Kenwyn's parish on the brow of the hill above Truro.

There had been bishops in Cornwall in the early days, but in 1047 King Edward joined together Devon and Cornwall in the Western See with its seat in Exeter, and there it remained for centuries. The ecclesiastical ferment of the early nineteenth century aroused hopes that Cornwall might once again have its own bishop, but it was not until 1877, after many appeals, that a diocese became established, and Truro was chosen as the cathedral city. Thus was the diocese born, without a cathedral, and without a residence for the first bishop, Edward White Benson.

The vicar of Kenwyn had already been warned as early as 1857 that his vicarage might one day be required for a bishop, but this did not cause him any dismay, since he was finding his 'expenses increasing and his receipts diminishing'. Kenwyn vicarage, 'more like a country house than a parsonage', had been remodelled in the Queen Anne style, and was described by John Wesley, who had once lodged there as the guest of a sympathetic vicar, as 'fit for a nobleman, and the most beautifully situated of any I have seen in the county'. This was, however, in the opinion of Canon A.B. Donaldson,

> an exaggerated and misleading description ... [it was] inadequate for its purpose; for there is no real chapel, and quite insufficient accommodation for receiving candidates for Holy Orders and other guests

> *(The Bishopric of Truro 1877–1902*, 1902:58)

although he added, 'the place has many charms', as Benson's son describes:

> There was a sunny circle of turf with rose-beds, and a big old-fashioned summer-house with alcoves, its open front flush with the wall, and built out behind the shrubbery. Then the winding path led down through trees and shrubs to the house, to another lawn with flower-beds, where a great lime-tree, feathered down to the ground, and gave good shelter in summer time. Beyond the shrubbery was a large vegetable-garden, and beyond that again an orchard with bee-hives and white cob-walls.

> (A.C. Benson, *The Trefoil*, 1923:179)

He concluded rather patronisingly, 'the whole place, though fairly trim, was not in any sense smart'.

Benson was followed by George Howard Wilkinson, who founded the Convent of the Epiphany. His successor, John Gott, in 1891 was wealthy enough to solve the inadequacies of the former vicarage temporarily by purchasing for himself the mansion of

Trenython at Tywardreath. His successor, Charles William Stubbs, in 1906 realised that something permanent needed to be done to rectify the deficiencies of Lis Escop, and enlisted the help of E.H. Sedding, from a Penzance family of ecclesiastical architects, whose uncle John Dando Sedding had published a book, admired by Stubbs, on *Garden-Craft Old and New* (1891), which was to strongly influence Thomas Mawson and Lutyens in their garden design. Bishop Stubbs himself had been a keen gardener and horticulturist as a vicar, and had published a book, *In a Minster Garden*, about his Deanery at Ely.

Bishop Hunkin described 'the wisteria on the east front of the house, and a brilliant clump of mollis azaleas in a sheltered corner south-west of the great lime tree' as 'treasures' for which 'I think we have to thank Bishop Stubbs', although the overall impression of his reconstruction is perhaps more fully represented in the rather exuberant account by the secretary to his successor.

> It was in spring a miracle of daffodils trumpeting in
> the grass, of little blue scillas thrusting up tender spikes ...
> of bird-cherry and lilac in June, of a glorious and even
> famous rhododendron tree blazing in the foreground.
> Later, the borders flamed with azaleas, and in a certain
> round-walled spot there were roses in such profusion as
> made gathering a bewildering joy. Not a stony cranny
> but was filled with little Cornish ferns and pennywort,
> not a wall but had its clematis or magnolia. This was a
> dream garden, with the Fal winding its way sleepily to
> the open sea.

(M. Moore, *Winfred Burrows*, 1932:134)

Bishop Stubbs had retrieved the pinnacle of the spire from the old church of St Mary's, which had been demolished in building the cathedral, and used the capstone, with the cross which had surmounted it, as the gnomon of a sundial. Such was an ancient form of time-piece which, if set up properly, would indicate the hours, although removed to its present position beneath trees and wrongly orientated, this may not at once be apparent. Around the base there is an inscription, which, from its mellifluous verse, must certainly have been composed by the bishop himself.

High above busy Truro town
Of Mary's Church this topmost crown
Has borne through nigh a century's space
The holy rood of Christ's dear grace
Now in Lis Escop's garden ground
As sunlit hours go circling round
This shadowed cross shall make and bless
My days of leisured quietness

Alas, the successors of Bishop Stubbs lacked his enthusiasm for gardening, so that Bishop Hunkin found it, so his gardener tells, 'in a mess'.

Upon taking up residence in Lis Escop, the Bishop made an immediate decision in favour of horticulture. The writer of his obituary in the *Gardeners' Chronicle* recounts that 'he told us that he had to chose between a chauffeur or a gardener, and his decision to drive himself and employ a gardener was characteristic of him.' Thereafter he drove about in a little Morris 8, somewhat erratically so his biographers suggest!

We may now safely leave the Bishop to describe his own garden in the following articles, and pass on to the eventual fate of the original Lis Escop. His own words did not prove prophetic when he wrote that from the time of Bishop Stubbs, 'to whom his successors owe so much ... no Bishop of Truro has wanted to change his residence or ever will.' Not so: Edward Robert Morgan, his immediate successor, took himself off to a smaller, though in the opinion of many, an unsuitable house in the Kenwyn Road, which had at one time been a vicarage of St Mary's Truro. John Maurice Key, who followed him, consequently built a new 'Lis Escop' on a plot of land on the Trelissick estate, which, although with alterations to suit the taste of each incumbent, has served ever since.

On the original Lis Escop being vacated, the Cathedral School, which was in need of larger premises, through the benificence of the Copelands of Trelissick, was able to purchase the property, which was forthwith renamed 'Copeland Court'. William Blakey, Bishop Hunkin's gardener, was retained to maintain and preserve as much of the grounds as were not used for school extensions, and the walled garden, so I was told, in those days was always full of vegetables and fruit.

The demise of the school in 1982 led sadly to an inevitable splitting up of the grounds into saleable smaller plots, which has

3   Bishop Hunkin with his gardener, W.T. Blakey.

obliterated the walled garden, and overrun much else. Some mature
trees remain, although the heavy storms in the late 1980s made
inroads into the woodland which had served as a windbreak. The
vacant house then became the residence of a much depleted number of sisters from the Convent of the Epiphany, who, as I write,
have declined to just two, who have now departed from the former
bishops' residence, whose future is at present undecided.

The horticultural writings

Bishop Hunkin had been a diocesan for seven years, and already an
accomplished theological author before, in 1942, breaking new
ground by writing an article in the *Journal of the Royal Horticultural
Society*. The question arises why, at that late stage in his career, he
should have begun, and continued increasingly to write on horticultural subjects.

We have seen that Bishop Hunkin's interest in natural science and botany was already formed before his return to Truro, which is demonstrated by his determination from the outset to take up gardening seriously. Yet he was still at this time innocent of any practical experience in horticulture. But added to his botanical interests and gardening determination, was his innate ability, already recognised in other studies, to grasp new knowledge swiftly, and to concentrate his mind at every available moment on the matter in hand. He himself acknowledged that he had the benefit of good teachers, in Canon Arthur Townshend Boscawen, rector of Ludgvan, an authority on tender, and especially New Zealand plants, and John Charles Williams of Caerhays, a good churchman, and probably the greatest Cornish gardener of his generation. Both men were closely in touch with the Royal Horticultural Society (RHS), to which they were able personally to introduce their friend and bishop.

The first article, on the Lobb brothers – the celebrated Cornish plant collectors for Veitch's Exeter nursery – is characteristic. The quest originated in taking advantage of an episcopal visit to Devoran, where Thomas Lobb was buried, to search the parish registers for information about the family. Even so, the purpose of the article was as much to announce that a subscription was being raised to erect a memorial tablet, as to record the results of his researches.

The next two articles, on Canon Boscawen, in the *Journal of the Royal Institution of Cornwall* in 1942, and on J.C. Williams in the *JRHS* in 1943, are more in the nature of memorial tributes to friends who had recently died, than specifically gardening articles, although the character of the two men made it inevitable that their interests and activities in horticulture would feature largely in his appreciation.

It was at this juncture that the first exclusively gardening article appeared in *The Guardian*, which was probably elicited by the editor, as its title suggests, to brighten the dark days of wartime, from a writer already known to the paper who was beginning to show an interest in gardening. It was no doubt this reputation, together with his association with such well-known Fellows as Canon Boscawen and J.C. Williams, which led the RHS that same year itself to invite Bishop Hunkin to address them on the history of Cornish gardens.

The address, divided into two parts, was published in the Society's *Journal* with the title, 'A Hundred Years of Cornish Gardens (1840–1940)'. It was the first of Bishop Hunkin's major horticultural articles, and exhibits to the full the distinctive quality of his writing – the meticulous scholarship with which he approached every subject he treated. Here he wrote from personal knowledge on the ground, together with the fruits of his researches, which included references to Cornish entries in Curtis's *Botanical Magazine*, and concluded with a comprehensive, if selective bibliography. The article remains the classic account of the status of Cornish gardens during this period. No such survey in this detail had been attempted previously, except for Charles Gilbert's desultory notes on the previous century in the second volume of his *Historical Survey of Cornwall* (1822). The list in Thurston's *Trees and Shrubs of Cornwall* (1930) is perfunctory by comparison.

Other articles were to follow, but since there is a descriptive Bibliography at the end of this book, little more needs to be said here, other than to focus upon two in particular.

The Bishop could claim some connection with an ancestor on the Isles of Scilly, where it was his custom to take three or four weeks' summer holiday, while conducting the Sunday services. This gave him the opportunity, as a 'vacation exercise', to browse in the library of the Abbey where at that time were housed a set of the valuable *Botanical Magazine*, and probably back copies of, at least, the *Gardeners' Chronicle*, if not other of the influential nineteenth century horticultural journals. The Abbey gardens themselves were also a source not only of pleasure, but of information to an enquiring mind, which could be supplemented by reference to the collection of standard, and some rarer horticultural authorities in the house.

This deep interest in the Tresco garden led first to a descriptive article in *The Guardian*, and then two years later to his stunning list of plants in flower on New Year's Day 1947, published in the *Gardeners' Chronicle*. However, this was just the sort of article that, to the superstitious, would be deemed 'tempting Fate', and indeed it was followed by a devastatingly icy winter. Fortunately, the Bishop was able to report in an article in the *Chronicle* later that year that the losses were not as great as feared, and another in *The Guardian* had the optimistic title 'Recovery'.

These ephemeral articles remain of interest, but it was the Bishop's masterly two-part article, 'Tresco under Three Reigns', which, like his account of Cornish gardens, remains of permanent value. It needs hardly to be said that it received the same scholarly attention as the earlier survey. Unlike the mainland gardens, however, there had grown up by this time an extensive literature on the Abbey garden, as a consequence of its unique nature, but little of it went beyond listing exotic plants, accompanied by superficial, and increasingly stereotyped facts about the origins of the garden. Bishop Hunkin's article was the first to trace the historical development of the garden using original documents, and first-hand information. The article also included a descriptive perambulation around the grounds, of which the Bishop, as in similar walks around Kew and other places, was a master. A similar walk was included, later that year, in one of the little 'Footpath Guides'.

Finally, I cannot leave this subject without making some comment on the Bishop's small handbook, *Trees and Shrubs for Cornwall*. It arose from Arnold-Forster being delayed by pressure of essential work from publishing what was to become his classic *Shrubs for the Milder Counties*. Arnold-Forster was an acknowledged authority on tender plants, who in 1938 had already written two articles on the subject in the *New Flora and Sylva*. It is surely significant that, when the local branch of the Council for the Preservation of Rural England (CPRE) looked for someone to produce an interim handbook, the Bishop was chosen, showing that he was considered to be the most capable of filling the gap. The booklet, which was widely welcomed among gardeners, is a model of its kind, which would not disgrace a professional horticulturist or nurseryman.

The Guardian articles

The Guardian, a church weekly, had been founded in 1846 after the secession to the Roman Catholic Church of J.H. Newman and others, to uphold the older traditions of the Oxford Movement. L.E. Elliott-Binns – a canon of Truro and the author of *Religion in the Victorian Era* (1946) – described the paper as 'the high-water mark of Anglican journalism', and another more literary historian wrote that it was 'long the organ of serious churchmen', aiming to provide independent comment upon theological, political and social issues. It is not surprising then that in 1951, the year after the last of the gardening articles, when a new breed of post-war clergy and churchmen had sprung up, that the paper folded, allowing the *Manchester Guardian* newspaper to contract its title simply to *The Guardian*, which in the present context can cause some confusion.

Although from the outset an Evangelical – a position he never forsook – Bishop Hunkin's independence of mind, and sometimes controversial political and social views, were not out of tune with the later years of *The Guardian*'s history when it had gained a reputation for 'liberalism'. Hunkin himself belonged to that pre-war generation of 'serious churchmen', many, if not most of whom had been educated at public schools and the older universities, where they had studied Classics – the last gardening article was printed alongside a sermon delivered in Latin with no translation! – or Modern subjects, and thus had broader interests than theology. Although there was a vigorous church life in towns and cities, the Church still had its roots in the countryside. This was the audience addressed by Bishop Hunkin in his articles – cultured and literary, with some, like himself, acquainted with the natural sciences.

All this may seem forbidding to a present-day reader. But this would be to leave out of account Bishop Hunkin's distinguishing – and endearing – characteristics of friendliness and homeliness. The articles are companionable pieces, conversational in style, with a lightness of touch and charm. Although proud of his Cambridge background, when writing about early botanists, who were clergymen, and sons of his old University, he finds space to tell us that Stephen Hales 'used to teach the housewives in his parish to place an inverted tea-cup at the bottom of their pies and tarts "to prevent the syrop from boiling over and to preserve the juice"'. He relates with evident glee that Adam Buddle (after whom the *Buddleja* is named), invited a botanist to look over his fine collection of plants 'where you will likewise meet Mr. Stonestreet [another botanist] and a great leg of country pork and peas for dinner.'

He puts on no airs. In one of his earliest articles he begins by describing how he was looking out for a place to eat his 'sandwich supper' after 'a tedious long journey on a summer's day in a crowded train' – from Truro perhaps – ending up sitting in the 'bomb-ruined churchyard of St James's', Piccadilly. Weary after a long conference at Lambeth, he takes himself off to Kew – in his Kew articles you feel almost as if you are walking beside him – where, in a quite natural way he strikes up a conversation with one of the working gardeners, whom he discovers to have spent the war as a cook in the North Sea fishing fleet, and who, after some regrets, declared himself glad to return to gardening at Kew. He adds, 'His contentment was infectious, and the rest of my walk in the garden I enjoyed more than ever.'

It is not clear how the articles came to be written, although, as we have seen, there was already an earlier tradition for series of gardening articles in *The Guardian*. To visualise the true picture we need to think ourselves back in time – the war was not over in 1943, and there was a weariness with restrictions. Light seemed a long way off down the tunnel. Time then perhaps for encouragement, and looking to the future. The great resurgence of popular interest in gardening in the immediate post-war years stemmed from the war-time 'Dig for Victory' campaign, when even those with only a back yard were encouraged to grow vegetables. In the Bishop's second article, when lamenting that Bishop Compton's garden after 1713 'had given way to the more ordinary products of the kitchen garden', he added, 'The last phrase may strike a sympathetic echo in the mind of the war-time gardener of today.'

If we can reconstruct in our imagination the mood of those days, we can appreciate better the sensitivity and tact with which the Bishop wrote his war-time articles. Perhaps the first of them strikes the right chord – 'Bright Shrubs for Dark Days' – a letter, as it were from the peace of the countryside to those in bomb-stricken towns, showing that life still continues, and beauty still survives. The following articles looked back to fine gardens in times past, interspersed with his own vision of scarred London (some of us can still remember the experience with wonder), of the rose-bay willow-herb colonising the heaps of bomb-site rubble. It was not until February 1944, when the possibility of the end of conflict looked nearer, that for the first time, he describes planting a few shrubs at Lis Escop, as if in a new flower garden. Indeed, perhaps it was, for he mentions a border 'for the moment occupied by war-time tall artichokes'. It was not until the war was really over, that the long series of notes on the ornamentals growing in 'my garden' were written. It would not have done, least of all for a bishop, to write glowing accounts of his garden, when his readers were tightening their belts, and scratching about to grow vegetables. The scene at Lis Escop in February 1944, then, may well have been an authentic relaxation of restrictions, since the great majority of the gardening articles come from after that date.

The final article, 'The Year Fades Out', was not published in *The Guardian*, but in *The Cornish Guardian and Gazette*. Nevertheless, from the acknowledgement at the foot, it is clear that it was written for, perhaps commissioned by, *The Guardian* itself. Just as the title of the first article had reflected the mood of the mid-war years, so too the title of the last was surely prophetic of the tragedy which a mere week or so later was to shock the diocese. Still, years later, for those who bear any affection for Bishop Hunkin, it makes poignant reading, so that it is understandable that *The Guardian*, rather than printing it in a national weekly, released it to be read by those in his own place, and among his own people. Nothing can form a more fitting end to this Introduction than to quote the opening words from the paper.

> The Bishop wrote the following article, 'The Year Fades Out' about a week before his death. The wreath for the service in Truro Cathedral, made by his gardener, who was also his friend, was composed of every plant that he had mentioned, down to a sprig of nut catkin. The unconventional material made a wreath of great beauty, with a cluster of pale pink blooms of 'Christmas Cheer' in the middle surrounded by a mosaic of colour. It was placed with the ashes in the sanctuary during the service and was later carried to the south aisle where, after the words of the committal, it was laid beneath Dr Hunkin's final resting-place.

The text of the articles

The articles have been transcribed from photocopies of the originals in the Library of Lambeth Palace, London, to whose Librarian I am especially indebted.

It was my original intention to print the text just as it is in *The Guardian*, but soon I came upon the inescapable difficulty in all garden articles written some time ago, which is the ever-changing names of plants. To leave them as they were would, I believe, risk the criticism of the purist, unless a tedious appendix of synonyms was provided; yet to add the changes within brackets would break up the flow of the text. Bishop Hunkin himself, as might be expected, always used the correct current botanical name for his plants, although sometimes ruefully noticing those that had not been settled. So there seems little doubt that, had he himself prepared his articles for the publisher, he would have brought the botanical names up to date. Consequently, I have followed the same course of action, without further comment.[2]

At present the Latin botanical name is customarily printed in italics, with only the genus beginning with a capital letter – cultivars, on the other hand, are in normal type within single quotation marks. Whenever the full botanical name, or the genus alone with a capital letter, or a cultivar is referred to in the text, it has been emended to conform to current usage. When plants are mentioned only in passing, however, their orthography is left as in the original, which, it needs to be said, is not itself always consistent in these matters.

In order to assist in the identification of plants where the botanical name is incomplete, or a common name is used which might not be immediately recognised – the Bishop occasionally had his own names for plants – I have made the necessary additions within square brackets, which are also used to surround all other editorial comments.

---

1 His biography, *Cornish Bishop* (1977), has been written by Alan Dunstan and John S. Peart Binns.
2 I have used the RHS *Index of Garden Plants*, 1994, as a reference.

Acknowledgements

My most grateful thanks must go first to Bishop Hunkin's son and daughter for their approval of the publishing of this book, and for supplying two family photographs of their father in his garden. The picture of Canon Arthur Townshend Boscawen was the Bishop's own, and was first printed in his article on the Canon in the *Journal of the Royal Institution of Cornwall*, in 1942.

I must also express my appreciation for the Foreword by the Bishop of Truro, and for his permission to use the diocesan arms.

The County Record Office were kind enough to allow the schedule of Memorial Plants, which is in their keeping, to be reproduced here. The list of plants in Lis Escop garden, however, has been enlarged and edited, but I am indebted to the Diocesan Office for supplying me in the first place with a copy of the original.

DOUGLAS ELLORY PETT
TRESILLIAN, TRURO, 2001

The Guardian Articles

In a Cornish Garden

Bright Shrubs for Dark Days

Early in January I took one Sunday at a country church where the living was vacant. One of the churchwardens was quite apologetic about the flowers: they were the fresh surprising pink of *Rhododendron* 'Nobleanum'. I thought to myself that his standard of floral decoration must be astonishingly high.

But standards are high here in Cornwall. On Christmas Eve I set out with a little offering consisting of a few sprigs of deliciously-scented wintersweet [*Chimonanthus praecox*] from a wall in my garden, eked out with some bright yellow of winter jasmine [*nudiflorum*]. I intended to take it to an old lady of ninety who has been a very great gardener. Actually I gave it to someone else on the way; and I was glad I did, for I found the old lady's room a perfect bower of flowers, the most striking object being a bough (I could call it nothing less) of *Hamamelis mollis*, its bare leafless wood glowing with its curious bright filaments of little fragrant blossoms. Here is a shrub for rectory gardens. I have a young one struggling on, all the more striking by reason of the lichen which is making too free with its branches.

Much more vigorous with me is *Daphne odora* against a southeast wall. Part of the wall fell down upon it during a gale a year or two ago, but it did not seem to mind; and every winter it fails not to give an abundance of its charming little pink and white bouquets of flowers with the sweetest scent in the world. I suppose it is tender, but I doubt if it is as tender as is commonly thought.

Nor, of course, are camellias. The flowers of a great healthy bush of *Camellia saluenenis* in the famous garden of Ludgvan Rectory are just getting over. The trouble is that they are so liable to be spoiled by winter rains and storms. The best plan, therefore, is to pick the buds, which will then open delightfully in water indoors. The name *Camellia*, it may be remembered, is in honour of George Joseph Kamel, a member of the Society of Jesus. He latinized his name into Camellus, and under it wrote an account of the plants of the island of Luzon in the Philippines, which he had visited. This account was published by John Ray, the Puritan, in an appendix to his great work, *Historia Plantarum* (1704). So does this gentle art of gardening bring Papist and Protestant together!

Another plant that is giving most welcome racemes of lemon-yellow flowers just now is *Mahonia bealei*, an evergreen of stiff and sturdy habit. It is quite hardy, though it does not like being moved, and its flowers have the fragrance of lilies of the valley.

I have mentioned only one species of rhododendron, but at Caerhays on the south coast I suppose a score of species are now in flower. One of the best of winter-flowerers is rose-purple R. *mucronulatum*. I have not got it, but one of my predecessors planted a fine bed of R. x *praecox* now covering itself with a mass of purple flowerlets.

Some Cornish gardens have *Acacia baileyana* flowering well in the open this mild year. I have a particularly pleasing form of it, but it is under glass. Last year its golden riches were prodigious on Christmas Day. It is flowering again now.

But for general utility winter-flowering let me commend some of the heaths, for example: *Erica carnea* 'King George', dwarf and deep pink; *Erica lusitanica*, ten to twelve feet high, introduced into Cornwall by a former Rector of Lamorran, the Rev. the Hon. John Townshend Boscawen, about the middle of the last century, its flowers pink and white; *Erica* x *darleyensis*, another smaller heath, which flowers so freely as to be a cushion of rosy pink.

(*The Guardian*, 19 February 1943, p. 66.)

Henry Compton

A Gardening Bishop

Three hundred years ago, in 1643, Spencer Compton, second Earl of Northampton, was killed at the battle of Hopton Heath in the Civil War. Thirty years later, in 1673, John Evelyn heard his youngest son, Henry Compton, by this time forty-one years of age and Canon of Christ Church, Oxford, preach at Court. "This worthy person's talent", Evelyn noted, "is not preaching, but he is like to make a grave and serious good man." Before the end of the following year, Henry Compton had so far become "a grave and serious good man" as to be consecrated Bishop of Oxford (December 6, 1674), and in December 1675, he was translated to the see of London. He exercised a good deal of personal influence at the Court of Charles II, and prepared the king's nieces, the Princesses

Mary and Anne, for confirmation. Later on he officiated at their weddings, and they both remembered him always with affection.

Bishop Compton was very sympathetic towards the Protestant Dissenters, and a strong opponent of the Papists. It is not surprising that he came to clash with James II, and in September, 1686, he was suspended from the exercise of all episcopal functions. The temporalities of his see were, however, according to the Common Law, the bishop's freehold, and he retired to Fulham, and threw himself with eagerness into his favourite botanical pursuits.

In the seventeenth century Londoners took a great interest in gardening. The last of the three celebrated gardeners, all called John Tradescant, grandfather, father and son, died in 1662, and their tombstone is still to be seen in Lambeth churchyard. The famous Physic Garden in Chelsea was founded in 1673, only two years before Compton became Bishop of London.

The bishop was not left to his gardening very long. In September, 1688, his suspension was reversed, and he plunged back into politics. In December of that year he escorted the Princess Anne for safety to Oxford as colonel of a little regiment of volunteers. He entered Oxford at their head "in a blue coat with a drawn sword", preceded by a standard bearing the motto *Nolumus leges Angliae mutari*. James II used to say that he talked "more like a colonel than a bishop". Next year (March 31, 1689) he crowned William and Mary. After that, he gradually became less prominent. To his great disappointment he was more than once passed over for the Primacy, and he continued at Fulham until he died in 1713 at the age of eighty-one. Opinions differed as to his efficiency as a prelate, but there was never any doubt as to his generosity. Indeed, he gave away most of his money and died a comparatively poor man. Whether he ever married or not appears to be uncertain. His wife, if he had one, was never in evidence.

The bishop's practical interest in botany was widely recognized by his contemporaries. John Ray's great *Historia Plantarum* (1688) includes descriptions of fifteen rare plants from the bishop's specimens in the Fulham Palace garden (vol. ii. pp. 1798, 1799); and a few years later James Petiver engraved a number of them.

Most of these plants the bishop had obtained from correspondents in North America. Among them were the tulip-tree (*Liriodendron tulipifera*), said to have been introduced into England by the Tradescants; the black walnut (*Juglans nigra*); the box elder (*Acer negundo*); and the poison ivy (*Toxicodendron radicans*). The tulip-tree, when fully-grown, produces masses of fragrant tulip-like yellowish flowers, but is chiefly prized for its stateliness and its fine foliage. The black walnut grows to as much as a hundred feet, with a wide spreading head and a tall dark trunk. Its leaves are fragrant when rubbed, but its nuts are of no value as food. The box elder is a handsome sugar-yielding maple. The poison ivy is remarkable for the beautiful red tints of its autumn foliage and for its poisonous yellow sap, which turns black on exposure and, because of its indelibility, makes one of the best possible marking-inks.

Before long the bishop's garden at Fulham gained the reputation of containing "a greater variety of curious exotic plants and trees than had at that time been collected in any garden in England". These words are a quotation from a paper read to the Royal Society on June 27, 1751, by Dr., afterwards Sir William, Watson, himself called by his friends "the living lexicon of botany." Watson had gone to Fulham Garden to see what was left after forty years of the bishop's plants. His short paper (*Philosophical Transactions*, xlvii, 241–7) contains a list of thirty-three exotics which he found there, but he was disappointed not to find more. "As the successors of this bishop in the see of London", he writes,

> were more distinguished for their piety and learning than for their zeal in the promotion of natural knowledge, the curiosities of the garden were not attended to, but left to the management of ignorant persons; so that many of the hardy exotic trees, however valuable, were removed to make way for the more ordinary productions of the kitchen garden.

The last phrase strikes a sympathetic echo in the mind of the war-time gardener of to-day.

Among the trees mentioned by Watson were the honey locust (*Gleditsia triacanthos*), with its beautiful fern-like foliage which turns bright yellow in autumn; the locust-tree (*Robinia pseudoacacia*), with feathery leaves and white racemes of flowers in June; the shapely sugarberry (*Celtis occidentalis*)[1]; and the spice bush (*Lindera benzoin*), whose leaves when crushed emit a pungent spicy odour. All these had been introduced into England from North America in Bishop Compton's time.

Watson's list also includes the cluster pine (*Pinus pinaster*), now so common at Bournemouth, and singularly picturesque when old

– with its dark, deeply fissured trunk bare for two thirds of its height; the strawberry tree (*Arbutus unedo*) – that exceptionally attractive evergreen with its strawberry-like fruit; and the Judas tree (*Cercis siliquastrum*), cultivated in England since the sixteenth century, sun-loving and delightful, with its bare branches covered with little rose flowers in May. The traitor Judas must indeed have been in despair if, as the legend is, he hanged himself upon this tree in the springtime. For the purpose of this brief account these must suffice. Dr. Watson pays tribute to the bishop's interest in "propagating botanical knowledge", and to his generosity in "communicating plants and seeds" to other gardeners, both in England and on the Continent. It would seem that gardeners have had more regard than ecclesiastics for the memory of this "grave and serious good man."

(*The Guardian*, 30 April 1943, p. 147.)

---

1 The 'sugarberry' is *C. laevigata*; *C. occidentalis* is the 'hackberry'.

A Parsonage Garden

Fifty Years Ago at Bitton

Correspondents in "The Times" have pointed out that the early emergence of butterflies links this year in a rather remarkable way with the year 1893. Actually, the winter of early 1893 was exceptionally severe, and the spring was exceptionally dry. In Cornwall most of the blue gums (eucalyptus) were killed by the frost; and the drought had a very damaging effect on the holly-trees, but the oaks produced a particularly fine crop of acorns. From March to May that year there were eleven weeks of bright sunshine, with dry easterly and north-easterly winds. The effect of this dry spring was discussed in the pages of *The Guardian* by Canon H.N. Ellacombe, Vicar of Bitton, who had been asked, three years previously, by the then editor, Mr. D.C. Lathbury, to contribute a series of articles on gardening. These were subsequently collected in two volumes: *In a Gloucestershire Garden*, published in 1895, and *In My Vicarage Garden and Elsewhere* (1902). Canon Ellacombe continued to be a regular contributor to *The Guardian* for nineteen years.

The parish of Bitton must be almost unique in having been served by two vicars, father and son, who between them covered a century all but one year. The father, the Rev. H.T. Ellacombe, began his work at Bitton in 1817; in 1850 he was succeeded by his son, who remained there until his death, eleven days before his ninety-fourth birthday, in 1916.

It was a very devout household in the vicarage, and Canon Ellacombe's third sister, Jane, was one of the two first women to join Dr. Pusey's first sisterhood. The canon himself, to the last, even when his age had compelled him to leave most of the parochial work to an assistant curate, always prepared his candidates for confirmation one by one. In one of his last letters, when he was over ninety-three, he wrote "I am getting on very pleasantly with my thirty-eight candidates. I shall have had about one hundred interviews by the end of the week, and a good many more before the 30th. I enjoy it much. It has not the least fatigued me – they are all so good."

Bitton vicarage garden covers about an acre and a half in a sheltered position on the west side of the Cotswolds, and there could have been no other garden of that size in the country which contained more interesting plants. The following are examples: the beautiful purple-pink stonecrop, *Sedum pulchellum*; *Yucca rupicola*; and, from the canon's famous collection of species of *Rosa*, the bluish-pink French *Rosa* x *alba* 'Incarnata', the lovely yellow banksia rose (*Rosa banksiae*, and the sweet white *Rosa luciae*, of prostrate habit, from China and Japan. These plants, grown in the Bitton garden, furnished the material for plates in the great *Botanical Magazine*, and no fewer than fourteen others sooner or later did the same.

As a gardener Canon Ellacombe was adventurous. "After all, you know", a friend once said, "Ellacombe's successes are due chiefly to his impudence." It is encouraging to a beginner to read in one of his letters: "If I had now one-tenth of the good plants I have had and lost, I should have a splendid collection."

Among Canon Ellacombe's favourites were the black pansy brought from Italy by his father; wintersweet (*Chimonanthus praecox*), whose fragrant blossoms he would enclose in his letters in the winter; the cheddar pink (*Dianthus gratianopolitanus*), which grew splendidly without the least attention on his high south wall; *Magnolia stellata*, covered with flowers of dazzling white; and the Japanese orange, *Poncirus trifoliata*, which fruited beautifully in 1893. Canon Ellacombe had made a standing offer to "the village maidens and marriageable ladies" that if they would find the husbands he would supply the orange blossom.

But to return to the spring. In May the garden was burnt up, and everything was thrown out of its proper season. The may was in full flower at the same time as the blackthorn (April 13). There was a wonderful abundance of flowers everywhere, but they were starved and dwarfed. The lily-of-the-valley was sadly deficient in scent, the late daffodils came with short stalks and small flowers. This year again (1943) has been an early year, but the spring had followed a mild winter. There have been times when we have been rather short of rain, but not seriously so; and I don't think I remember, for things in general, a better flowering spring.

(*The Guardian*, 4 June 1943, p. 184.)

In a London Churchyard

Rose-bay and London Plane

After a tedious long journey on a summer day in a crowded train, I took a bus to Piccadilly, and looked about for a place where I could eat my sandwich supper. I found a battered garden-seat in the little bomb-ruined churchyard of St. James's in front of the shattered church: and there I sat in the sunlight of the early evening. All around me were the tall, handsome rose-coloured spikes of the Rose-bay or Bay Willow Herb, looking as though they had deliberately come to adorn and cheer the ruins. It is a rock-loving plant, growing on barren, stony hillsides, and its tiny brown seeds are provided with a tuft of long, white silky hairs at the upper end which serves as a parachute. They are thus wafted down into crevices where they find a lodgment, and spring boldy and readily up when summer comes. So, wind-borne, they hasten all over the country to the rescue of waste and barren places, and gladden the eyes of child and man. A weed? But what a splendid weed: *Epilobium angustifolium*, its technical name, owing to the fact that its flowers appear to rest on lobes and its leaves are narrow – called Blooming Sally sometimes in Ireland, where *Sally* is a corruption of the Latin *salix* (willow).

But if Blooming Sally has flown to cheer the city after the blitz, the London plane has been there all through it. There is no stouter-hearted tree. Bombed and broken, it soon hides its scars under its broad, green leaves and heals its wounds with fresh growth.

In point of fact, the plane proved itself in London long before the war. In spite of smoke and fog, asphalt and paving-stones, it is a picture of health and happiness. The upper surface of its leaves is smooth and firm, and a shower of rain easily washes them clean, while the bark flakes off and changes itself year by year. The leaves are perhaps rather late in appearing, and it is not until the month of May that they unfold from their buds. Both male and female flowers are collected into tight-packed little globular clusters, the former about the size of peas, the latter larger (about half an inch in diameter).

When the female flowers have ripened into fruits, these fruits hang on the tree all through the winter, and may even be observed as late as April. In the autumn the leaves turn shades of gold or reddish brown, and fall somewhat later than those of most trees.

Three planes that rejoice me perpetually are the beautiful trio on the little plot of grass just north of Henry VII chapel, Westminster Abbey. One of the many merits of the tree is that grass grows freely under it.

There is little grass left in Berkeley Square, where the oldest planes in London are, but that is not the fault of the trees. Now that the railings are down, you can see all the uniform burry trunks swelling at the base – a fine plantation filling the centre of the Square; the two tallest must be over a hundred feet in height. This, according to tradition, was a burial-ground during the Great Plague in 1665. The trees were planted by Mr. E. Bouverie in 1789.

There are two main varieties of plane, one originally from Greece and Italy; and one from North America. The latter (*Platanus occidentalis*) was introduced in the first half of the seventeenth century, but it is short-lived, rather tender, and uncommon. The former, *Platanus orientalis*, has been in England since the middle of the sixteenth century. There is a fine old example in the bishop's garden at Ely. It was planted by Bishop Gunning (1674–1684) on a low hill fifty feet above the fens, sheltered on the north and east by buildings. Towards the end of the nineteenth century it showed signs of failing, but it was top-dressed with good soil and regained its health. It is over a hundred feet high and more than twenty feet in girth.

The tree at Ely, however, is not exactly the London plane. It is [the typical] *Plantanus orientalis*. The origin of the London plane itself is somewhat obscure, but it is believed to be a seedling variety of *P. orientalis* which has been fixed in cultivation, *Plantanus orientalis* var. *acerifolia* – so called because of its maple-like leaves. It was first distinguished in 1703, and in that century it became common. It may well be regarded as a symbol of the cheerful toughness and buoyancy of the City of London, whose tree *par excellence* it certainly is.

(*The Guardian*, 20 August 1943, p. 272.)

Parson Hawker

Further Recollections of Morwenstow

The parish of Morwenstow, the most northerly of Cornish parishes, stretches along five miles of rocky coast. The population at the last census was reckoned at 584. A hundred years ago it was over a thousand. At that date its vicar was Robert Stephen Hawker, best known for his ballad of six verses including the four lines:

> And have they fixed the where and when?
> And shall Trelawny die?
> Here's twenty thousand Cornish men
> Will know the reason why!

The ballad first appeared anonymously in *The Royal Devonport Telegraph and Plymouth Chronicle*, September 2, 1826. It was hailed as a genuine ancient ballad by Sir Walter Scott, Lord Macaulay, Charles Dickens, and a number of other writers. But Hawker later stated that he wrote it under an oak in Stone Wood in 1825, and that the only ancient lines in it were the last three of the verse quoted above. These, he said, had been a popular proverb throughout Cornwall ever since the imprisonment by James II of the Seven Bishops, one of whom was Sir Jonathan Trelawny, Bishop of Bristol. There is some reason, however, to suppose that the lines are earlier still, and were used in connexion with a grandfather of the bishop's, John Trelawny, one of the leaders of Charles I's party in Cornwall, who was committed to the Tower by the House of Commons in May, 1627, and released after about a month's imprisonment.

Hawker wrote the ballad at the age of twenty-two. Five years later he won the Newdigate Prize at Oxford with a poem on Pompeii. This poem attracted the attention of Bishop Phillpotts, and indirectly led to the bishop's offering him the living of Morwenstow, which he accepted in 1834, and where he remained till his death in 1875. Meanwhile, as an undergraduate at Oxford, Hawker had married a well-educated lady twenty-one years older than himself. After her death in 1863, he married, at the age of sixty, a young woman of twenty. Both marriages were happy. Neither put a stop to Hawker's eccentricities. On December 30, 1863, Miss Kuczynski, at that time a governess in a family living in the parish, wrote in her diary: "Mr Hawker, our vicar, is slightly cracked – but he's a very clever old soul." On December 21 of the following year she married him in Holy Trinity church, Paddington. They had three children and the husband of one of them, Mr. C.E. Byles, published in 1905 the most authentic of his biographies – *The Life and Letters of R.S. Hawker.*

Out of his first wife's money Hawker built the present substantial vicarage. He chose as its site a spot where he had seen the sheep take shelter in a storm. The tablet he set over the front door may still be read:

> A house, a Glebe, a Pound a Day;
> A Pleasant Place to Watch and Pray.
> Be true to Church – Be kind to Poor,
> O Minister! for evermore.

The annual value of his rent-charge was £365, but this was at a time when the wages of farm labourers in the parish were seven or eight shillings a week. If modern incumbents had incomes twenty times that of farm labourers (whose minimum is now £3), they would be rolling rich indeed. Happily these gross inequalities no longer exist. As a matter of fact, "Parson Hawker", as his parishioners affectionately called him, was very free with his money, impulsively generous to those in need, and often in financial difficulties himself. He spent large sums in restoring the church, and in building and maintaining the school – Morwenstow still has a Church school, and a very good one.

There were many shipwrecks on that iron-bound coast. "I have this day buried my thirtieth sailor in the Seaman's Burial Ground by the Upper Trees", Hawker wrote in a letter dated November 12, 1862. The sole survivor from the wreck of the Caledonia of Arbroath in September, 1842, was Mr. Le Dain, a Jerseyman, whom the vicar took into his home and looked after for some weeks. When he returned to Jersey he used to act as Hawker's agent for getting Jersey cows for the glebe farm, which Hawker farmed himself. He was a very keen farmer, and was one of the first English clergymen to revive Harvest Thanksgiving as a Festival. On September 13, 1843, he issued an invitation to his parishoners:

> Let us gather together in the chancel of our church on the first Sunday of the next month, and there receive, in the bread of the new corn, that blessed sacrament which was ordained to strengthen and refresh our souls ... Let us remember that, as a multitude of grains of wheat are mingled into one loaf, so we, being many, are intended to be joined together into one, in that holy sacrament of the Church of Jesus Christ.

He further fortified his exhortation with quotations, which incidentally illustrate his somewhat erratic use of Holy Scripture. His concluding words were as follows:

> Brethren, on the first morning of October, call to mind the word, that wheresoever the body is, thither will the eagles be gathered together. "Let the people praise thee, O God, yea, let all the people praise thee. Then shall the earth bring forth her increase, and God, even our own God, shall give us His blessing. God shall bless us, and all the ends of the earth shall fear Him."

It is the centenary of this invitation that we celebrated at Morwenstow on Sunday, October 3, and I took as my text those last two verses of Psalm 67.

By 1860, Harvest Thanksgiving had become general throughout the country. The harvest hymn, "Come ye thankful people come", was published by Dean Alford in 1844, and some of the harvest favourites date from the early sixties: "Praise, O praise our God and King" (1861): "We plough the fields, and scatter" (1862): "To Thee, O Lord, our hearts we raise" (1864); "The sower went forth sowing" dates from 1874.

Hawker continually raged against Dissenters. The bulk of the people in his parish, he said, "had become followers of the great preacher (John Wesley) of the last century who came down into Cornwall and persuaded the people to alter their sins" – the bulk of the parishioners of Morwenstow are Methodists still. Personally, however, Hawker was very friendly with them. "I like to give them

a little comfort in this world", he used to say, "for I know what dis-
comfort awaits them in the next."

It is interesting to reflect that the famous High Church Vicar of
Morwenstow was a contemporary of the famous Bible Christian
preacher, Billy Bray of Baldhu, converted in November, 1823; both
men ardent Christians, both with a touch of genius, both with
accompanying eccentricties. The two never met: but on one occasion (in 1847) Hawker was visited by the Rev. W. Haslam, the Vicar
of Baldhu, whose "conversion" so rejoiced Billy Bray that he
danced round the table. And Haslam was greatly impressed by his
visit. "This friend", he wrote, "was a poet, and a High Churchman,
from whom I learned many practical lessons ... He persuaded me to
wear a priestly garb like his, and gave me one of his old cassocks as
a pattern; this I succeeded in getting made to my satisfaction, after
considerable difficulty." So, though Billy Bray never saw Hawker, he
probably saw his own parson arrayed in a Hawker cassock.

(*The Guardian*, 8 October 1943, p.329.)

At Lis Escop

In the Garden after Epiphany

The period just before and after Christmas had been unusually
busy. There had been pastoral letters to write for Lent, and a pam-
phlet on confirmation; several institutions; and, in addition to the
usual services, a number of extra ones to help with. For, like every
other diocese, we are getting very short-handed. In Cornwall young
clergy are always few: now, of course, there are fewer than ever. At
an early celebration in the cathedral not long ago, the average age
of the three clergy present worked out at nearly eighty.

But on the day after Epiphany I had no public engagements. I
put on a soft collar – those hard collars are the worst part of the
clerical uniform – I devoted myself to tidying up. A consignment
of plants from Marchant's, Wimborne, was expected. A postcard
had announced its despatch on January 4. It is now January 7, and
my friend and gardener, William Blakey, had spent the greater part
of the day in preparing ten spacious pits for the ten new-comers. In
the afternoon I rang up the station. The plants had arrived, a large
parcel in sacking of 86 pounds weight, to be delivered the follow-

ing morning. But to-morrow might be wet: I decided to fetch the package myself. I had another errand in that part of the town, and drove the car to the station. With the assistance of a porter, I fastened my precious burden to the back of the car, a slender cone ten feet high tapering to a point. I drove slowly home and deposited my prize in triumph. Gardener had the water-tank ready in the stable yard. The plants were beautifully packed, and in splendid condition. We plunged their roots in water for a few minutes, and then set to work. It was getting on for five o'clock, but before dark we had finished.

4 Bishop Hunkin in his garden.

First we went to a corner just below the sweep of the drive in front of the house. There were two places ready for two plants of sea buckthorn (*Hippophae rhamnoides*), a male and female to ensure a good harvest of orange-coloured berries in autumn. Sea buckthorn is very accommodating, and no special preparation of the soil had been necessary.

Next we wheeled the barrow to the main lawn, where, in the shelter of a large rhododendron, a round hole was waiting for the greatest treasure of all, a pink flowering dogwood (*Cornus florida* f. *rubra*). I had been advised to go to Marchant's for this most attractive little tree by one of the greatest of living authorities, Mr. C.P. Raffill, of Kew. In due course the tree will, I hope, be covered with masses of bright rose-red fowers in May and June, and in autumn with glorious shades of orange and scarlet.

Our next site was in a border, for the moment occupied by wartime tall Jerusalem artichokes. Here very careful preparations had been made for two camellias, *Camellia oleifera*, the only scented camellia I know of. The soil had been enriched with leaf-mould, and the beds raised a little above the surrounding ground to facilitate drainage. These lovely Chinese plants in a sheltered position in Cornwall should give their five-petalled white flowers from November to February.

From this border we went to the far garden, where there is a remarkable view over cathedral and estuary, with wooded hills beyond. Here we are preparing a little arbour, and at the back of it we planted two of the prettiest and most fragrant of escallonias – 'Donard Gem' and 'Slieve Donard'. Of all shelter plants near the sea, I put escallonias first, and I have great hopes of these two.

Finally, back in the afore-mentioned border, among the tall stalks of Jerusalem artichokes, in three good pits symmetrically arranged, we put three fine upright plants of *Viburnum betulifolium*. One day I hope they will form a solid group which will provide an avalanche of bright red berries, untouched by birds, and shining for weeks in autumn and winter.

After the scene of the Epiphany we get no picture of our Lord until some twelve years later. I should like my friends to visit Lis Escop garden in twelve year's time. By then all my ten fledglings should have their feathers. I hope they will be a joy to my successor, and to his successor too. Those who plant in one of the church's gardens should plant for a far-stretching future.

(*The Guardian*, 18 February 1944, p. 62.)

Cornish Gardens

A Week-end of Flowers

The third week-end of May was for me a veritable week-end of flowers. It began with a christening in a country church on the Saturday afternoon. It was a charming old building, mercifully short of stained glass, and bright with sunlight. Along the top of the font the vicar's wife had placed a broad spray of fresh ivy, and in it at intervals little tight bunches, some of buttercups and some of daisies. My eyes were drawn again and again to the buttercups. They were solid yellow, unbelievably shining. What could have been more fitting for an infant baptism? And the hymns were to match: "Once in royal David's city", and "Loving Shepherd of Thy sheep."

After the service, the christening tea was held in a dining-room looking out on a long lawn with beautiful curving sides lined with banks of shrubs and backed by light woodland. After tea, we were taken down the grass paths by our kind host, one of the most skilled of Cornish gardeners. A number of rhododendrons were still in flower, though the early ones were over. They were remarkable shades of soft pinks and reds. The lovely great inverted cups of *Magnolia sieboldii* ssp. *sinensis* were dangling plentifully from their shapely tree. A *Davidia* [*involucrata*] from China was gay with white bracts fluttering like tiny pocket-handkerchiefs from its graceful branches. There were groups of blazing azaleas, of *Pieris formosa* var. *forrestii*, remarkable for its white lily-of-the-valley flowers, and still more for the marvellous brightness of its young red foliage, and one of the most interesting collections of enkianthus to be found in this country.

Next day, Sunday, on my way to a confirmation at Gulval, overlooking Mount's Bay, I went round a great garden in a neighbouring parish. It was here that that fine red rhododendron, discovered by Captain Kingdon Ward, first flowered in England – R. *elliotii*, and from it by skilful crossing had been created other first-class scarlets like R. 'Fusilier'. The distinguished owner is, indeed, a specialist in scarlet rhododendrons, and his brilliant masses are astonishing. He has a number of the more delicate scented rhododendrons, too, and gave me some branches of R. x *fragantissimum* to take away with me, and also a mighty and most fragrant flower-goblet of *Magnolia wiesneri*. Other beautiful things I caught sight of as I drove slowly down the long drive leading out to the lane towards Gulval: notably rich masses of shining brown and yellow broom.

Finally, after the confirmation, the vicar took me into the churchyard and there, behind the church, I saw a big Chilean firebush, *Embothrium coccineum*, with its amazing spangles of brilliant red. It is a beautiful churchyard in a wonderful situation, and, with its vicar a keen gardener, in a few year's time it will be more beautiful still. As I drove away; I thought of the contrast between first and last: those hardy and familiar buttercups, and that delicate stranger, the embothrium: both indescribably, and how differently, lovely. "He hath made everything beautiful in its time: also He hath set eternity in their heart." (Eccles. iii, II.)

(*The Guardian*, 13 June 1944, p. 228.)

A Garden at Ludgvan

Summer-flowering Shrubs

There can be no lovelier parsonage garden in the world than the rectory garden of Ludgvan, on the slope of Mount's Bay looking out to sea, with the romantic pile of St. Michael's Mount in full view. The garden was made by the late Canon Arthur Boscawen, Rector of Ludgvan from 1893 to 1939. Canon Boscawen was one of the great gardeners of the great gardening days at the beginning of this century, and in 1922 he was awarded the Victoria Medal of the Royal Horticultural Society, the highest honour the society has to bestow.

When I was there last on the afternoon of the first Sunday in August, the present rector and his wife, Canon and Mrs. R. de C. Murley, showed me one of Canon Boscawen's favourite plants at its best: a great column of white wide-open flowers – *Eucryphia* x *nymansensis* 'Nymansay'. This beautiful Eucryphia first appeared at Nymans, in Sussex, as a natural hybrid between two Chilean species. Its flowers are bowl-shaped, two inches and more wide, freckled with numerous yellow-tipped stamens. The *Eucryphias* do best under woodland conditions in soil free from lime.

Another plant from Chile is a great joy in my own garden at Truro throughout the summer: *Calceolaria integrifolia*. This is an evergreen shrub up to four feet high, extremely gay with a profusion of bright yellow pouch-like flowers. It needs protection during severe frost.

A similarly rewarding summer-flowering shrub is *Ceratostigma willmottianum*. Twiggy and compact, it freely produces its bright sky-blue flowers from May to October. It is a native of Western China, where Mr. H.E. Wilson found it in 1908. Two plants were raised from his seed by Miss E.A. Willmott, of Warley Hall, Essex, and from these the present stock in the country had been mainly derived. Miss Willmott was the first woman ever to be admitted as a Fellow of the Linnean Society (1904), and it is fitting that this delightful shrub should bear her name. It needs the sun, and against a sunny wall will grow to ten feet high.

A much easier plant to grow than any of these, and equally floriferous, is the Tree Mallow, *Lavatera arborea*. This handsome shrub is sometimes found wild in Great Britain – for example, on the Bass Rock. It grows up to eight feet in height and bears abundant purple-red flowers for weeks and months. I gave a plant to a camp on a very exposed site hundreds of feet up just above the sea on the North coast. It was planted near the main entrance, where it was blown about by every wind. But it throve most sturdily and covered itself with flowers; and the camp was very proud of it. It was the Vicar of Porthleven who very kindly gave me my own Tree Mallows, after I had admired them growing in his garden; and I would strongly recommend the shrub for the parsonage garden anywhere.

(The Guardian, 1 September 1944, p. 300.)

Gold Flowers for Epiphany

On the first Sunday after Epiphany, a drive of thirty miles took me to the fine church of St. Keverne, in the Lizard peninsula, where the churchwardens and their supporters were carrying on gallantly during a long vacancy. I was greeted by the cheerful ringing of the eight bells of the church tower. In the afternoon I went down to the sea for Evensong at Coverack. It is a beautiful little open cove, and the sea was a cold, calm blue, with the wind off the shore. After tea there was Evensong in St. Keverne church, still blacked out, for it stands high, and from the churchyard there is a wonderful view of the coastline, curving past the Helford river in a wide sweep to the great harbour at Falmouth, and far to the East beyond. After the service, there was the drive home over Goonhilly Downs and up the narrow lanes from Gweek to the Helston–Truro road. It was the first drive of any length I had had since undimmed lights were again allowed – and what a sense of relief they gave!

In the intervals between the services I spent some time going round the garden at Lanarth with its present owner, himself a keen gardener and the son of the man who made the garden, the late Mr. P.D. Williams, for many years people's warden of St. Keverne church. Lanarth garden, of some twenty acres, is one of the finest woodland gardens in the whole country. At that time of year it was, of course, mostly full of leaves and bare twigs. Of the latter, Mr. J.C. Williams of Caerhays, cousin and very close friend of Mr. P.D.'s used to say: "Thank Heaven, the flowers have gone, and the leaves are gone, and now I can see my trees." Many of the evergreens at

Lanarth are most shapely and beautiful, with leaves lovely in form and texture: *Lindera megaphylla* for example, the Chinese spice bush, here a charming little tree.

I saw a large *Rhododendron* 'Nobleanum' faithfully producing its trusses of cheerful pink. But the sight of the garden was a most magnificent Chinese witch-hazel, *Hamamelis mollis*. It is a great airy spreading bush, twenty feet high by twenty feet across. It has been given plenty of room in a sheltered place, and is thoroughly happy. This is the more remarkable, as its slender branches are clothed with lichen. Just then they were also richly adorned with little starry flowers of golden yellow; and the effect of these fragrant spangles of brightness lighting up the silver green tufts of lichen was simply marvellous. This, I said to myself, must be the loveliest Epiphany plant in England, if not in the whole world. Appropiately enough, by the side of it was a beautiful Juniper, *Juniperus recurva* var. *coxii;* from the fragrant wood of which the Chinese love to make their coffins; so that it is commonly known as the Coffin Juniper. What more could I ask to suggest the Epiphany association of gold and frankincense and myrrh!

There are four species of witch-hazel, all very hardy in Great Britain. The one longest known is a native of Eastern North America (*Hamamelis virginiana*), and was introduced into this country as early as 1736. Its leaves resemble those of our own hazel, and this resemblance led the early settlers in North America to use its branches as divining rods, and to call the little trees "Witch-hazels." There is another less-known American witch-hazel, but both of them have now been eclipsed by the other species from the far East, China and Japan. The Chinese *Hamamelis mollis*, is the finest of all, and presents a rich and perfumed offering of gold flowers for Epiphany. It gives me added pleasure to know that *Hamamelis mollis* was first described and figured from specimens sent home by that great plant collector, Augustine Henry, who, when I was an undergraduate at Gonville and Caius, Cambridge, became a senior member of the College. He was collecting hundreds of new plants above the Ichang gorges about the time when I was born; and he found *Hamamelis mollis* in the Patung district of the province of Hupeh. The number of specimens, dried and labelled, sent by him to Kew over a period of fifteen years, is said to have amounted to 158,000!

The witch-hazels are not the only plants that give us yellow flowers for the Epiphany season, as St. Keverne church itself reminded me. In a shallow bowl near the entrance to the chancel were little bunches of violets and sprigs of yellow gorse. This is not, of course, the proper flowering season of that wonderful generous plant, but still it contrives to produce sprays here and there to offer at Epiphany.

Nor must I forget my dear old friends in the garden at home, Winter-sweet and Winter-jasmine – not golden perhaps, but the former richly fragrant and the latter radiant and gay: and last of all, Bailey's Mimosa, than which there is no more beautiful *Acacia*, with its elegant feathery leaves and its crowded flowerheads of bright lemon-yellow. I planted it a few years ago under glass, where it has flourished amazingly and threatens to lift off the roof of the little green house. There, this year, it opened without heat on the very Feast itself, Saturday, January 6.

(*The Guardian*, 2 February 1945, p. 43.)

High Lights of May

The Cornwall Garden Show at Truro has been suspended during the war. We look forward to it again next year. It is always held in April, and it is from April to May that the great Cornish gardens are at their best. This year things have been exceptionally early throughout the country. On the Sunday of the National Thanksgiving (May 13) I was at Saltash with the Vicar of St. Stephen's and a kind parishioner had sent him strawberries for tea from his garden just south-west of the Tamar.

In Lis Escop garden the high lights of May are the wisteria on the east front of the house, and a brilliant clump of Mollis Azaleas in a sheltered corner south-west of the great lime tree. For both these treasures I think we have to thank Bishop Stubbs (1906–1912), to whom his successors owe so much. His predecessor, Dr. John Gott, found Lis Escop inconvenient, and moved to Trenython, looking out over the sea above Par. Into that house he built his two pillars from the Temple of Diana at Ephesus, and there they are to this day – to the edification, no doubt, of the railwaymen whose convalescent home the house now is. Bishop Stubbs did a great deal for Lis Escop, and since his time no Bishop of Truro has wanted to change his residence or ever will.

The wisteria is *Wisteria sinensis*, introduced into England from a garden in Canton about a hundred and thirty years ago. Its slender twining branches carry pinnate leaves and long racemes of very numerous lilac-blue flowers. Their fragrance floats in at the bedroom windows on the first floor. I am reminded of another wisteria in the garden of Mr. E.A. Bowles, of Myddelton House, Enfield, one of the greatest gardening authorities of our time, who is also a distinguished lay-reader and has this month celebrated his eightieth birthday. This wisteria is twenty years old and climbs along a wall and up an ancient yew to the height of forty feet. The whole expanse of the plant is most impressive, and at a glance it might be taken for some gigantic blue laburnum. On one occasion, indeed, someone admiring it from the road was heard to say to his companion, "That is a blueburnum."

Last year, at another corner of the same side of the house, I planted another wisteria, which I hope will soon grow up to meet it. This is *Wisteria venusta*, whose shorter racemes of white flowers are still more strongly scented. It has made an excellent start, and at the top has produced one flower already (which must, in so young a plant, speedily be removed).

Wisterias are easy plants to grow and quite hardy in the South of England. Places like Oxford and Cambridge have many of them, and should have more. A wisteria is the sole plant of note in the beautiful old court of Dr. Caius at Cambridge. As you enter the Gate of Honour you see it in front of you, and to the right in the corner by the Master's Lodge.

At Lis Escop we have half-a-dozen groups of azaleas, and, indeed, no plants are more suited to the soil and climate of Cornwall. They belong, of course, to the great rhododendron family, and want an acid soil. A rough test is the presence of bracken: where bracken will grow, rhododendrons will grow. The azalea section of the family has been greatly developed in recent years. There are the early Mollis Azaleas in great variety, with the Occidentale hybrids a little later, and the famous Knap Hill hybrids with their fiery colours. All these are deciduous, and give fine effects of coloured leaf in autumn. Many of the evergreen azaleas come from Japan and smother themselves with flower. Among the more familiar are the varieties of the Obtusum Group which hide leaf and twig and everything else under a glowing cushion of warm pink in spring.

Our most striking group is Bishop Stubbs' bed of about a dozen Mollis Azaleas to which I have already referred. They are old plants now, some of them from eight to ten feet in height, dazzling the eye with flaming orange and red, and spreading far and wide a rich spicy honeysuckle fragrance. The flowering will be over before the end of the month, and as in peace-time the diocesan conference garden party generally comes at the end of June I have planted a bed of later varieties. It is too early yet to report on them. They have settled down and just show their colours: *Rhododendron arborescens*, fragrant flesh-pink flowers, and the swamp honeysuckle, *R. viscosum*, with flowers of a still paler pink and stronger fragrance, both from North America. I have hopes that they will be good, but I can see already that Bishop Stubbs' group will long remain by far the best.

So much for Lis Escop garden, but the light of all the lights of May I saw in Falmouth parish church on the evening of Whitsunday. The flowers were red and white in accordance with the season, and the red were the brilliant scarlet spangles of *Embothrium coccineum*, the fire-bush of South America. For the tongues of fire of Whitsun no shrub or tree can touch this rather tender and tempermental Chilean beauty. It was introduced into England about a hundred years ago by a Cornish plant-collector, William Lobb, and appropriately enough, it flames its brightest in Cornwall. This year has been a good year for it, as indeed for all flowering things, both great and small: Nature having put on her most glorious array to give thanks with us for victory.

(*The Guardian*, 8 June 1945, p. 220.)

Flowers in Church

It is abundantly worth while taking pains over the selection and the arrangement of flowers in church. There is great scope here for anyone with a flair for decoration, and flowers both familiar and unfamiliar can be used with notable effect. Very likely the flowers will be remembered when the preacher, and even the choir, are forgotten.

Three recent examples linger in my mind. They are all connected with institutions to benefices. In this diocese, a diocese I think of just the right size with about 220 benefices, the bishop is able to take all these institutions publicly in church. They are happy occasions, with a little tea-drinking and a few words from the church wardens and the new incumbent afterwards: not without surprises – as when one patron, presenting his nominee at the beginning of the service, addressed me as "Reverend Father in Heaven"!

Early in June I drove to Menheniot in the rain, a long and dreary drive, to institute an Army chaplain, just returned from the Near East. It is an Exeter College living, among whose incumbents have been such men of distinction as William of Wykeham in 1365 and Peter Courtenay (1529–1554), who is said to have been the first in those parts to teach and catechize in English, the Cornish language having till then been used. The whole complexion of the evening changed for me as I stood before the large congregation in the fine fifteenth-century church and looked at the altar decoration: white pinks, dark red single roses, and small branches of *Kalmia latifolia*, the North American laurel. They were perfectly lovely; and at the chancel steps there were tall earthenware jars containing more *Kalmia*, with glossy dark green leaves and a profusion of dainty, porcelain-like pink and white flowers, which give it its name of *calico bush*. The calico bush was introduced into England by a Quaker, Peter Collinson, in 1734. Mr. Bean, of Kew, says that it is probably the most beautiful evergreen shrub ever obtained from Eastern North America. It is quite hardy, and I wonder why we see so little of it in this country. In the Arnold Arboretum in Massachusetts a great breadth of it between two and three hundred yards long provides a feast for the eyes every June. I have an old-established plant in Lis Escop garden, and not long ago I put in some more, which have made a good start. There are one or two fine bushes of it in the vicarage garden at Luxulyan. It likes peat and loathes lime, and keeps good company with rhododendrons.

Two days later I was at another institution, in the tiny church of Trevalga with a Norman font. It was a sun-shiny afternoon with a stiff breeze, making white horses gallop on the blue sea far below us. The altar decoration was simpler, but it rejoiced the heart. It consisted of delicate creamy-white spikes of spirea, with dark pinks, against the background of a black curtain.

The third institution took place towards the end of July in another little church with a Norman font, St. Thomas by Launceston. Again there was a good congregation, and a fine turn-out of the neighbouring clergy to welcome their new brother. The scheme of decoration was, this time, quite different. On a ledge behind the Holy Table were four vases, the two outer larger, the two inner smaller. In the outer vases were tall daisies with long thin white petals, feathery green sprigs of asparagus, and red antirrhinums, with one dark phlox to match. In the inner and smaller vases were blue cornflowers, orange-yellow marigolds, and red carnations. The list sounds as though the effect might have been a jumble. Far from that, the array was bright and light and delightful.

Sometimes, of course, it is better to have flowers in a tall vase on a stand a little in front and to the side of the altar. And one country church I know where you find fresh flowers all round the church any spring or summer day you look in. It is a light church, not gloomied by the ordinary or sub-ordinary stained glass, and the flowers make it always gay and welcoming. Would there were more like it! But here the vicar is a good countryman and not a bad poet – a combination admirable, but rare.

(*The Guardian*, 17 August 1945, p. 322.)

Tresco Abbey Gardens

In June, 1879, at the opening of the church in Tresco, the most beautiful of the Isles of Scilly, the first Bishop of Truro, Dr. Benson, referred to a petition sent by the monks of Tavistock to the Bishop of Exeter in the fourteenth century asking that their two brethren stationed at their small outpost at Tresco might be replaced by secular clergy. The Isles of Scilly were dreadful places, they said, and there was nothing going on there except robbery and piracy and frightful weather.

The modern history of Scilly begins in 1834, when Augustus Smith, of Ashlyns, near Berkhamsted, obtained a long lease of the Isles from the Duchy of Cornwall in succession to the Dukes of Leeds. The latter had been absentee landlords, and the islands had fallen on evil times. They had become over-populated; former industries, like the laborious making of kelp from the seaweed, were coming to an end, and the more remunerative enterprise of smuggling had been drastically curtailed, if not altogether suppressed. Augustus Smith, as Lord Proprietor of the islands, acted with great vigour. He built piers and roads and schools. Education he made compulsory in Scilly long before it was compulsory on the mainland. The children had to pay a penny a week if they came to school, twopence a week if they stayed at home. The Lord Proprietor encouraged the new industry of building of small ships which was just beginning, and set a good example himself by starting a farm at Tresco on up-to-date lines. He gradually built himself a house near the ruins of the ancient abbey, and he established in bold outline the great garden.

First of all shelter had to be provided. When Augustus came to Tresco there was no plant on the island bigger than a large bush. He built a wall to give his young plants a start, and put in a large number of trees, both the hardiest deciduous trees he could find like elms and sycamores, and also, and more as time went on, conifers.

The climate of Scilly is mild. The temperature rarely falls below 40 degrees or rises above 60 degrees. The number of hours of sunshine is about the same as that in Guernsey. There is a good deal of rain and mist. But the main enemy is wind. In the winter of 1929–30, for instance, there were no less than fourteen occasions when the wind rose to over eighty miles an hour. Augustus was successful in planting the side of Tresco hill, which gives a certain lee from the western storms. *Cupressus macrocarpa* was one of the principal trees he used to good effect.

From the first the Tresco garden was unlike any other in the British Isles. Augustus made good use of the rocks and great stones of the island, and he obtained plants from a number of places nearer the Equator which gave his garden an unusual, semi-tropical, appearance. Some of these plants he had from Kew, but more were brought back by captains sailing from Scilly, or sent to him by his friends overseas. He was particularly fond of the fig marigold, *Mesembryanthemum*, of which he had scores of varieties: his "mesmerisms" he called them, with their thick succulent leaves and starry flowers, large and small, of glistening white, bright yellow, red and purple. He had massive hedges of red geraniums, great bushes of fuchsias, acacias covered with yellow blossoms, belladonna lilies, verbenas, cinerarias, irises, ixias, nemophylla, aeoniums with their rosettes of fat green from which spring stalks of bright flower, correas, hebes, genistas, bamboos, sparmannias, azaleas, sennas. Imagine his delight when the large variegated aloe in front of the old abbey emulated, as he said in a letter, Jack's beanstalk, and shot up its amazing mast of flower; or when the evergreen metrosideros first covered itself with scarlet; or when the beschornerias produced their blazing red stems; or when the puya, from Chile, put up its spikes more than nine feet from the ground and formed its great heads of shining yellow. Among the other plants which Augustus specially mentions are *Pittosporum tobira*, with its beautiful cream scented flowers; the palms, *Trachycarpus fortunei*, and *Chamaerops humilis* var. *arborescens*; and *Hakea suavolens* from Australia.

Augustus was very kind in allowing visitors to come freely into the garden. They would be a bore, he writes, in 1861, "did they not really seem to enjoy themselves and appreciate the place and its peculiarities; some fifty were here this week in a body, from all parts of the Kingdom, of whom a few were really learned in plants, to Chivers's (his head gardener) great satisfaction." The Scotch, he says, "are the most intelligent, as shown by their questions and observations; the Cornish the least so, and who, when he [points] out some botanical rarity, answer, 'Well, that's not so good as a cabbage.'"

Augustus was a firm Churchman, and the sort of parson he approved of is indicated in his description of a Mr. Hartwell who arrived at Tresco in September, 1851: "Our new spiritual pastor and master arrived here the last week in September. Mr. Hartwell is a well-seasoned, sound minister, of some twenty years' experience in the Church; a well-informed, gentleman-like man, and the most simple-minded creature in the world, performs the service simply and earnestly, and preaches admirably; all plain roasted and boiled, without sternness, imbecility, nonsense, ignorance, or eccentricity."

Augustus died in 1872, and was succeeded by his nephew, Thomas Algernon Dorrien Smith. Thomas Algernon's rule in Scilly was on similar lines, but milder. It was he who started the commercial cultivation of the narcissus in the islands. The 'Scilly White' and the 'Soleil d'Or' he found growing about the abbey ruins. Possibly they had been introduced by the monks. As an experiment he sent up a hat-box of the flowers to Covent Garden, and realised £1 for them. The first flower show to be held in the Isles of Scilly took place on Tuesday, March 30, 1886, when Thomas Algernon showed upwards of a hundred and sixty varieties of narcissus arranged on a groundwork of green moss.

Meanwhile he had been developing the abbey garden. He discovered that *Pinus radiata* (*insignis*) stood the wind better than *Cupressus macrocarpa*, and he was able to establish a belt of shelter on the south-west side of Tresco hill. The plants in the garden continued to flourish and grew larger and larger. Some which Augustus had never seen in flower came into blossom in the 'seventies and 'eighties. *Furcraea longaeva* was one of the most striking of these. From a yucca-like base it shoots up a very tall stem with slender branches bearing its cream cup-like flowers. The *C. macrocarpa* along the abbey drive formed itself into a huge hedge of unusual beautiful green 50 feet high, which it took a fortnight every year to clip.

Thomas Algernon died in 1918, and the present owner, his eldest son, Major Arthur Dorrien Smith, D.S.O., succeeded him. The major had already made his mark in the horticultural world, and particularly by introducing from the Chatham Islands the finest of all the olearias: *O. semidentata* with its great, lovely, purple daisy-like flowers. He had travelled extensively in South Africa, Australia and New Zealand, and had sent and brought to Tresco a large number of seeds and plants of various kinds. Most fittingly he was, last year, awarded the highest honour of the Royal Horticultural Society, the V.M.H.

And so the great garden has survived wars and storms, and still extends its warm and generous welcome to all comers to-day. As you walk along its terraces, stretching east to the west on the south slope of Tresco hill, you will find the quiet air laden with an unfamiliar spicy fragrance from the scented leaves of the bright pelargoniums massed along the paths, the great eucalyptus trees here and there in the background, and the beds of dark purple heliotrope. Now, in early September, most things are over; the echiums, for instance, and the many crassulas, except a big crimson one lingering here and there. But there are still hebes white and blue and purple, agapanthus blue and white, masses of gay mesembryanthemum, an excellent white jasmine, some lovely rich abutilons, orange, white and crimson, *Bursaria spinosa*, covered with white feathery blossoms, a beautiful great purple convolvulus, many trees of *Clethra arborea* with its lily-of-the-valley-scented white flowers. The bottle-brushes, the aloes, the banksias and many other exotics, though not at present in flower, and the great strange glossy foliage of the *Meryta sinclairii*, the sacred tree of the Maoris, *Brachyglottis repanda*, and the like, all contribute to the stately distinction of the garden. Most impressive are the dicksonias or tree ferns, the great palms, *Phoenix canariensis*, and the huge *Metrosideros excelsa* with its hanging roots reaching towards the ground. A long row of these metrosideros form a broad line of scarlet in July which can be seen far out to sea, and present, perhaps, the greatest spectacle of the whole year.

The flowers in church come, of course, from the great garden; and I shall not forget the magnificent effect of pink belladonna lilies with branches of *Clethra arborea* one Sunday at the end of

August. In that little church on Sunday, August 19, we followed, with the dean's kind approval, the form of service used on VJ-day in Westminster Abbey. So was the centre linked with the circumference in thanksgiving. And, indeed, Tresco has not been behindhand in the sacrifice through which the victory was won. Three of the major's four sons were killed in action. The Dorrien Smiths are a brave and adventurous and public-spirited family. Long may their line continue to serve their King and country and the Church of God!

(*The Guardian*, 5 October 1945, pp. 387,390.)

An Open Christmas

On the evening of the fourth Sunday in Advent I drove home through sheets of rain. The day before had been wet and windy too, and it was not surprising, for the barometer had been as low as I ever remember seeing it. Christmas Eve was a much finer day. We had the usual carol service of Nine Lessons in the cathedral church. The first Bishop of Truro, Edward White Benson, drew up this service, which is now widely in use throughout the country; and here in Truro we keep more closely than elsewhere to its original form. The cathedral is a grand place for it. There is space, stateliness and good singing, with copes and candles, the Christmas tree with a star shining at the top, and the Crib with the lantern in the stable; and as dusk draws down the soft lights shine out the brighter.

Instead of Christmas cards I gave the boys of the choir an apple each from the best apple tree in Lis Escop garden, and to the men I presented buttonholes, also from the garden. Next morning on the breakfast table there were buttonholes for the whole household. Staff and family, ten souls in all, breakfasted together, and we all wore buttonholes of the same pattern. Each was built up on a sprig of *Skimmia* with its dark shining green leaves and bright red holly-like berries. To this were added a couple of pieces of a rich purple heath, and one of wintersweet for fragrance, with its little yellow florets on the bare twig.

The day was mild and bright, and after we had returned from Morning Prayer my wife and I walked round the garden and counted the shrubs which were in considerable flower. There were just over two dozen. Along the lower path a group of *Hebes* from the Isles of Scilly still showed their rich blue-purple. At the top of the drive a *Mahonia* had made a good beginning with its fragrant drooping panicles of creamy yellow. In the far garden a *Genista* was in full bloom and was matched by a bank of *Coronilla valentina* ssp. *glauca* nearer the house. On both sides of the centre walk flowering shrubs were out. A *Camellia speciosa* was covered with buds, and some of the buds had opened into lovely pink cups; not far from it a young *Camellia oleifera* was flowering for the first time. Its white buds have a charming pink flush, and it is supposed to be fragrant, though the fragrance was not yet apparent.

On the same border one of the best of the St. John's Worts, *Hypericum* 'Rowallane', was still presenting its great blossoms of butter-yellow, and by the grass on the other side were two bright purple cushions of heath, with a tall and ancient tree heath behind the bamboos beginning to open its thin sprigs of white. The tender *Buddleja auriculata* was still bearing its pale scented flowers, and there were several little fuchsias in bloom – the sort which has the tiniest little purple flower bells. Our *Correas* from Scilly have stood out for two or three winters, and now they are full of their tubular flowers, one of pale lemon-yellow, and the other gayer in rose-red. We have two early rhododendrons ('Nobleanum' and another) both showing considerable flower, one pinkish white, the other a very fresh bright pink. *Grevillea rosmarinifolia*, with its rosemary-like leaves under which nestle its soft red filaments of flower, is very reliable with us, and seems to be out most of the year. And of course *Viburnum tinus* and the winter jasmine never fail us – or anybody else.

On our best wall, a high wall of old red brick pleasantly curved and facing south-east and south, our trusty winter-sweet is now the most outstanding plant. It is very large and full of vigour. Last year it was drastically cut back, and now it shows its gratitude for the kind attention by supplying us liberally with those charming little blossoms to which I have already referred. More surprising on the same wall is an *Abutilon*, offering its inverted bowls of brown-orange, and a *Brugmansia* with its long hanging pitchers of a similar colour. This *Brugmansia* has a wonderful vitality. Frosts cut it to the ground, caterpillars devour its leaves, we remove its roots, and yet year by year it comes again undaunted.

Another bush which covers itself with flowers (tiny white stars) for months together is a New Zealand *Leptospermum* by the wall of the drawing-room. It is still well out: and so is the autumn Prunus, though our specimen is young and delicate-looking. *Cassinia fulvida* also has not yet ceased to show its terminal corymbs of small white flower-heads.

In this list I have not counted the odd flowers on the *Ageratina*, the Corsican lavender, the pink-white *Abelia*, one or two pink-red spiraeas, our small *Garrya elliptica*, whose green tassels are not yet fully out; or the dozen buds, very late revellers in the rose garden. And I hardly like to mention the purple, scented, *Petasites* standing where it ought not, a most persistent weed, this year particularly floriferous. On wild banks it may deserve the name of winter heliotrope, but not in the garden.

The walk was a good preparation for turkey and Christmas pudding, and the family giving of presents around the log fire in the dining-hall, the singing of carols by the whole household, and finally a charade "featuring" national and local celebrities. Earlier in the day had come the news that some anonymous donor had put £100 in the offering at the midnight celebration of Holy Communion in a church in Truro which had been damaged in one of the "tip and run" raids during the war. This introduced an unexpected crescendo into the delight and thanksgiving of the most care-free Christmas for many years.

(*The Guardian*, 4 January 1946, p. 9.)

March Morning at Kew

There is the best authority for one day's rest in seven, and as the parson is busily as well as happily employed on Sunday he should make a Sabbath of some other day of the week. Monday has much to recommend it; and on a Monday morning in the middle of March I repaired to Kew. The weather had been cold for weeks but the wind had changed and it was mild and grey. The sky had a rather rainy look, but the barometer was high and I took my umbrella and set out for two or three hours in the Royal Gardens.

There were very few people about as I entered the Victoria Gate and looked across the pond in front of the Palm House. On the bank were three beautiful willows named appropriately *Salix* x *sepulcralis* 'Chrysocoma', "golden-haired", for they seemed to have mixed some sunlight into the tender green of their delicate drooping branches. On a tiny island nearby two tall swamp cypresses [*Taxodium distichum*] stood like sentinels above a clump of swaying bamboos. There are a number of these cypresses at Kew, and they are trees you turn to look at again, with their tall masts thickly surrounded by short branches of a rich brown colour all pointing upward. By another side of the pond a low mound under a spreading oak was carpeted with white and purple crocuses. A moorhen, I am sorry to say, was eating them. I glared at her and she slunk away ashamed, though I am afraid only for a few minutes, for I soon passed on.

What I specially wanted to see were certain trees: the southern beeches in their winter dress, and the bishop's pine. On my way to the spot indicated on the plan of the gardens I passed a shapely bed of the best forsythia (*F. intermedia* 'Spectabilis') just beginning to show its shining yellow flowers. Three species of southern beech (*Nothofagus*) I noted, and there are one or two others in the gardens. They are charming trees of a more slender habit than our own native beech but some of them up to 100 feet high. The three I looked at were all from South America, and the one I liked best was *N. procera* from Chile, a neat tree with delicate branches, now grown to a moderate size. A bluetit, hopping about on it, seemed pleased to see me. We certainly ought to grow more of these fine trees in Cornwall. Another tree, much less familiar, should be introduced into Great Britain far more freely. It is the *Zelkova* (*carpinifolia*) from the Russian provinces south of the Caucasus. There are several specimens at Kew, one over sixty feet high. The tree resembles nothing so much as a most elegant heavenly besom standing on its handle. It grows somewhat slowly but it is perfectly hardy.

Near the beeches I saw a couple of sweet gums (*Liquidambar styraciflua*) from North America. This beautiful tree was introduced into England by Bishop Compton who had it planted in Fulham Palace Garden in 1681. It is best known by its brilliant leaves in autumn. Through some mistaken idea of the durability of its timber it was used in 1907 for the paving of Whitehall. Actually the paving wore out so soon that it was the subject of famous lawsuit. Not far away from the sweet gums there was a very graceful weeping beech, and further, towards the lake, an elegant hornbeam of pyramidical form. There is something very neat and pleasant about a hornbeam, especially one, like this, of moderate size. As I approached the lake itself I came upon the alders. One was hung both with last year's fruit and also with the gay tassels which herald the approaching spring; and near them were three little Japanese birches (*Betula ermanii*), bright with fawn-pink bark. It happened to be one of the two days during the year when the lake is emptied in order that its banks may be cleaned. The notice "Paddling strictly forbidden" seemed unnecessarily peremptory on its placard standing out of the mud, but the waddling inquisitive ducks appeared to look me over with a friendly eye.

Not far away I found the bishop's pine (*Pinus muricata*). It is a hundred years ago this year that this pine was introduced to England from California. It was discovered at San Luis Obispo and named the bishop's pine after Bishop St. Louis. This particular specimen was of no great size and it was fully clothed with dense evergreen leafage. In California the pine grows to fifty feet or more, and in the Isles of Scilly and the Channel Isles it thrives in exposed situations. Its cones may remain unopened on the tree and still retain their seed for twenty or thirty years.

I was now making towards the bank of the Thames where the water was running rather low between the Garden and Syon Park. It was a peaceful and attractive vista with Syon House directly in front and the lion on the top of it so proud of its outstretched tail. When I turned back, near the nursery I found a group of eight wild [almonds] (*dulcis* var. *pollardii*), whose bright pink blossom was bravely recovering from the frost. Later, in another part of the garden, I saw a big *Prunus cerasifera* just beginning to sprinkle its dark green branches with small delicate blossom of creamy white. Another wild [almond] (*dulcis* var. *macrocarpa*) was gay with flowers whiter and larger. A peach (*P. persica*) I saw with plenty of tight buds not yet opened, and a corylopsis from Japan just beginning to expand its fat buds of cheerful yellow.

Undeterred by the warning "No Thoroughfare for Bath Chairs or Perambulators" I came upon the rich red of a quince against a wall. Against another wall *Viburnum farreri* was flowering freely, and on another *Magnolia grandiflora* was showing just one great pointed cream bud. In a border two plants of *Daphne mezereum* were covered with their small purple blossoms, and not far away a mediterranean heath was making a beginning with scanty buds of pink. In some places daffodils were opening in the grass, and here and there and very frequently the glory of the snow (*Chionodoxa luciliae*) self sown was brightening the ground with stars of blue and white.

As morning passed into afternoon slight sprinklings of rain alternated with fitful attempts at sunshine. I do not remember opening my umbrella, but I admit straying into the Temperate House. I was delighted to find that in spite of all the glass broken in the blitzes the house was filled – not to say crowded – with trees and shrubs in obvious health. There was a good deal of refreshing colour on the rhododendrons, the camellias, and a number of other plants. But of these I must say no more, for the object of my expedition was out-of-doors. To all my brethren, the clergy of the diocese of London, Southwark and Rochester, I warmly commend a Monday morning at Kew.

(*The Guardian*, 5 April 1946, p. 160.)

Cornish Gardens

Rhododendron Time

In the great garden at Caerhays, on the south coast of Cornwall near St. Austell, flowers can be found on some rhododendron or other in every month of the year. The flowering rises to its peak, however, in April. The Cornwall Spring Flower Show, which includes both daffodils and flowering trees and shrubs, is held early in that month. For many years before the war the first prize in the main class of flowering trees and shrubs was generally won by Canon A.T. Boscawen, whose garden at Ludgvan was perhaps the most remarkable rectory garden in England. Canon Boscawen had a brother in the New Zealand Forestry Service, who sent home seed of various kinds such as pittosporum, leptospermum, olearia, and hebe; Canon Boscawen's collection of New Zealand plants was the finest in the country. He did not, however, specialise in rhododendrons. It is to the other great Cornish gardeners of that generation, notably Mr. J.C. Williams of Caerhays, and his cousin Mr P.D. Williams, of Lanarth, not far from the Lizard, that the county owes the introduction of the magnificent rhododendrons which blaze in the larger Cornish gardens at this time of year.

The rhododendron is a rather sedate and serious-looking evergreen, and to see it smothered in large trusses of bright flowers on some spring morning against a blue sky is a revelation.

The Cornwall Spring Flower Show was not held during the war, but this year it appeared again in full strength. There were rows and rows of splendid daffodils, lines and lines of exquisite camellias, group upon group of astonishing magnolias, and a grand display (not for competition) of rhododendrons and azaleas from Caerhays. The most remarkable single object in the show was a stupendous truss of *Rhododendron macabeanum*, one of Captain Kingdon Ward's introductions from his 1928–1929 expedition to Assam. The truss consisted of large creamy flowers backed by the huge leaves of that class of rhododendron. It was taken from a plant in Mr. George Johnstone's delightful garden at Trewithen, near Grampound, the plant itself being covered with flowers, an almost unbelievable sight. This rhododendron is, of course, a species, one of the vast number which are found in the central home of rhododendrons which lies in that area where Tibet and China meet Burma and Assam.

Another species of a very different sort, much smaller and lighter, I was surprised to see outside the churchyard by the war memorial at St. Tudy, near Bodmin, one Saturday at the end of April, when I went to the village to institute the new rector. The rhododendron had been trained so that its slender standard form bore a great head of blossom of a delicate blue-purple. I recognized it as *Rhododendron augustinii*. It must be the only village in England to have its war memorial so graced. And in the church I saw on the ledge behind the altar vases of other lovely rhododendrons, of which I did not know the names. These were hybrids, raised by a great Cornish gardener, Captain E.J.P. Magor, who lived for many years in the parish of Lamellen. Lamellen has been in his [mother's] family since the days of Queen Elizabeth. There is a long drive winding up to the house, with slopes rising on either side lightly planted with fine oak, beech and other forest trees, giving the semi-shade that most rhododendrons love. Captain Magor added greatly to the beauty of these slopes by the judicious planting of a selection of the finest rhododendrons, both species, and also hybrids of his own devising. He used to give as his definition of an optimist a man suffering from *angina pectoris* who goes on sowing rhododendron seed (rhododendrons often take years before they flower), and he died of *angina pectoris* himself. Mrs. Magor (one of the thirteen children of a distinguished Cornish vicar, the late Canon Westmacott) very kindly took me down the drive that quiet Saturday afternoon and showed me its rare and glorious treasures.

Of these perhaps the most famous is a group of the tall and very graceful conifer, *Cryptomeria japonica*. Among the rhododendron species I remember specially the delicate pink flowers of *Rhododendron davidsonianum* in one of its best forms, and the largest *Rhododendron cinnabarinum* I have ever seen, covered with tubular flowers of bright cinnabar red, on a high bank above a little lake. Among the hybrids, there were plants of the finest blue rhododendron (I suppose) in existence. Mrs. Magor said it was a form of 'Blue Tit' (it looked like 'Blue Diamond'), of a rich dark hyacinth blue. Also by the path, and looking as if it were overflowering itself, I saw a medium-sized rhododendron laden with large trusses of a beautiful clear light pink. It was one of Captain Magor's own hybrids. I do not know whether there is another such in England (*thomsonii*, a small tree which covers itself with rich red bells, crossed by *detonsum*, a shrub of about the same height with flowers of rose-pink). Mrs. Magor said that the health of the plant required it to be drastically cut back, and she gave me a great branch which nearly filled the back seat of my little Morris 8, and I took it home in triumph to my astonished family.

Only the day before I had spent a long time in walking round another Cornish garden at Camborne. I was so interested that I did not realize how long it was; there were so many rhododendrons and magnolias to see. And of them all I liked none better than a bed of young scented rhododendrons in a sheltered corner. Rhododendron perfume has an exotic spicy delicacy that makes me think of what nutmeg might be but isn't. The queen of this fragrant corner was a small specimen of *Rhododendron taggianum*, a lovely white with a yellow blotch and a most delicious lily-like scent. If that tender beauty will really flourish there, it will be a triumph indeed.

(*The Guardian*, 24 May 1946, p. 241.)

Plants Respond

If a holiday-maker found himself in one of our English cathedrals on the afternoon of the first Saturday in August and stayed to Evensong, he would have heard read from the thirteenth chapter of the Gospel according to St. Luke the parable of the fig-tree growing in a garden. The owner said to his gardener, "See, this is the third year I have come to look for fruit on this fig-tree and cannot find any. Cut it down. Why should so much ground be wasted?" But the gardener pleaded, "Leave it, sir, this year also, till I have dug round it and manured it. If after that it bears fruit, well and good; if it does not, then you shall cut it down."

How should the story have continued? I have often wondered. I am inclined to think the tree would have brought forth figs and been reprieved. For the gardener was going to do the right thing. A fig-tree is liable to produce nothing but a luxuriant crop of leaves if it is planted in rich deep soil of unlimited extent. The gardener's digging would have the effect of root-pruning, and that is what the tree needed. Then when small figs appeared and set, a top dressing of farmyard manure would bring them on; and, if the owner knew about figs and did not gather them till they drooped with the skin slightly cracked, the juice standing on the surface like dewdrops and a large tear in the eye, there is no doubt that he would spare his tree.

In this garden I had an old fig-tree in a good position against a wall, but it persisted in doing so badly that at last I had it cut down. I have had several others planted, one in this same position. It is a Brown Turkey, and on it and another Brown Turkey in the open in another part of the garden my hopes are set. There are, of course, other varieties, and my friend Prebendary W.R. Johnson has been very successful with several in his rectory garden at the head of a little valley which affords him a modicum of shelter near the bare exposed coast north-east of Newquay. What exactly he does to please his fig-trees I am not sure. Fig-trees love moisture, and in his garden they have plenty.

The fact is, plants in general respond to kindness and good treatment. Some years ago I was given a nice little specimen of that very beautiful rhododendron, *R. edgworthii* [formerly *bullata*]. It was discovered by a French missionary in China the year before I was born, but not introduced into England until 1904. It has leaves with a puckered (bullate) surface, green above and thickly covered underneath with tawny felt; and its lovely flowers are deliciously scented. They are waxy-white with a yellow stain inside, and on the outside tinged with pink. I knew this rhododendron was tender, so I gave it a warm place in front of my best wall. To shelter it I also planted a short hedge of a quick-growing evergreen pittosporum from New Zealand with the pretty dark green leaves which are much sought after in Covent Garden for foliage. But the rhododendron was still too much in the sun, and this year I have moved it into the semi-shade of a shrubbery. Already it has responded with renewed vigour and remarkable fresh growth.

Shrubs which flower in late autumn are comparatively scarce and correspondingly valued. One of the most reliable in this garden from September to November is that hemp agrimony from Mexico, *Ageratina ligustrina*. It is an evergreen bush of dense growth and hemispherical shape, with bright pale green leaves and flower-heads composed of six to ten tubular florets, creamy-white with a slight rose tint and charmingly fragrant. Each winter I have been taking the trouble of cutting off the flower heads, and the response of the plant has been good to see. It is bursting with health and comeliness.

But I have come to the conclusion that what plants appreciate more than anything else is good food. Well fed, they seem to become much hardier and able to put up with cold and wind and generally detestable weather. *Abutilon vitifolium*, the abutilon with a vine-like leaf, is very different from the other abutilons or Indian mallows. It comes from Chile and bears lovely open five-petalled flowers in shape rather like those of a "single" holly-hock and of a beautiful pale purplish blue. I planted one of these abutilons in a corner below our tennis court, and another I gave to one of my helpers who has a small farm a couple of miles away. He planted his by his house with the farmyard adjoining. My plant has done but poorly. It had grown very slowly, and it is still only a single stem about three feet high, and has not yet flowered. But my friend's shot up amazingly. Though it was in a colder, more exposed position than my plant, it evidently found something from the farmyard in the soil which it enjoyed. Very rapidly it reached a height of fifteen feet, spread wide its branches and smothered itself in blossom. The contrast with my poor little specimen of the same age was most extraordinary.

Another example of the striking effect of exceptionally good food I noticed in some wild foxgloves which had seeded themselves in some of the garden beds. I like foxgloves, so I did not disturb them, and they grew and enjoyed themselves thoroughly. My gardener and I measured four of them; one was eight feet three inches in height, two were eight feet six inches and one was actually eight feet nine inches high.

This rainy year has been a wonderful growing year for plants in general. A tall friend of mine found a penny-pie two-thirds the length of his walking-stick. In some parts of this garden shrubs and trees are spreading out so far that it is a puzzle to know how to keep a path to walk in. *Magnolia* x *soulangeana* is an example. It is a low-spreading tree which flowered well in April, with its long vase-like flowers, white and purple, first on the bare shoots, and then continuing till June when the tree was full of foliage. This year it has pushed out so far over the path that it is difficult to get by it.

One of my skimmias is another example of unexpected growth. Last autumn it looked sickly; now it is covered with fresh green and has taken on a new lease of life. No doubt it will in due course produce its fragrant clusters of little white flowers and fine scarlet berries. Yet another example is afforded by our clump of *Rhododendron* x *praecox*. As its name implies, this rhododendron flowers early – at the end of February. Its foliage is of a refreshing deep green and its smallish flowers are of the brightest and most beautiful of purples. Our bed is a long-established one of about a dozen plants. One died earlier this year and we took it out, and my excellent gardener, whose song is often in the minor key, said that the whole clump was "going home". Since then, however, it has shown unmistakable signs of renewed youth, and we have given it a good mulching of well-rotted grass cuttings to which it will certainly give a further response. And how delightful it is to evoke response – vegetable, animal, or human!

(*The Guardian*, 23 August 1946, p. 396.)

Survivors of the Great Frost

A few days ago I was visiting an old friend at Cambridge, formerly for many years one of the most distinguished of the University's Divinity Professors. He is now eighty-five years of age, and he told me that he could never remember such a severe winter as that which is now coming to an end. Cornwall had escaped much more lightly than Cambridge, but even here we have had more snow than for fifty years, and on three occasions the thermometer in my garden has registered eighteen degrees of frost. The worst of it was that the snow came just too late, and the hard frost had penetrated far into the ground before it arrived. So that, instead of being a kindly protection, the snow cruelly blanketed-in the icy cold. There have therefore been very heavy losses, so heavy indeed that the Cornwall Spring Flower Show scheduled for April 10, has been cancelled.

But we must not be downcast over-much. Many of the plants which now look brown and dead, or, like my evergreen *Michelia* from the Himalayas, are stripped bare of every leaf, will probably come again from lower down. We had a short spell of devasting severity some years ago, during the late Canon Arthur Boscawen's last illness. From his bedroom window he watched the effect on his lovely rectory garden at Ludgvan. When he heard talk of cutting down a big plant badly scorched by the frost he made a tremendous effort to say something. He was so paralysed that he could hardly speak, but he shook his head and lifted his hand and his wife was able to catch the words "Leave it: it will come, it will come." And that is just what I propose to do now, hoping for the best.

Certain plants I know have gone: "gone home", as the gardeners say in these parts – I suppose it is an echo of some of the Sankey and Moody hymns. The Cornish are terribly fond of hymns. My old headmaster at Truro School used to say that they would not ride on the musical merry-go-round at the fair unless every tenth tune was a hymn tune!

But the list of my plants which have certainly departed this life is a sad one. Some, it is true, I do not deeply mourn: *Myoporum laetum*, for example, with its large neat head of shining leaves, is in place in the great garden at Tresco, but was never likely to fit in so well here. It was very rash of me to try to keep the South African *Crassulas*, with their fleshy leaves and charming crimson flowers, out-of-doors through a winter; and similarly the Australian Plume Acacia, which was given me in a pot by the rector's wife of Lansallos. A tall mast of a *Eucalyptus* we had recently moved because it was too near my *Magnolia stellata*, one of the best plants in the garden. It had moved unexpectedly well, but it is dead now and I am not surprised. But I am very sorry to lose some of my *Hebes* and *Leptospermums*, my Tree Mallows, and a number of young plants which I was nursing on. Never mind: there must have been a considerable mortality among the garden pests with which we have been wrestling for years; and some beautiful plants have stood the strain nobly. The first prize I would give to the Chinese Witch Hazel (*Hamamelis mollis*). All through these bitter weeks it has been wreathed in smiling blossoms. Little rosettes of yellow and brown filaments they are, close set on their thin brown sprawling branches. Next I would put one of my *Camellias*. It holds itself erect and its leaves are green and glossy as ever and it is full of flower. The flowers, as they open, are, it is true, browned by the frost. But pick the buds at an early stage and bring them indooors and they will open and last for weeks. They are cups of a rich deep pink with shining yellow stamens. One or two of the heaths are sturdy and reliable too, and cheerfully cover themselves with their familiar spikes of pink and purple. The *Daphnes* were surprisingly good, especially *Daphne odora*, pink and white and deliciously fragrant. The little *Rhododendron edgworthii* also came through unhurt. She is undoubtedly tender, but she only had a piece of sacking on the north-east side of her to keep off the worst of the wind. My *Rhododendron falconeri*, with its huge leaves brown on the underside seems none the worse, and shows great fat buds which I hope are still undamaged. My clump of *Rhododendron* x *praecox* gives promise of covering itself with its bright blue-purple, though it will be six weeks later than usual. My daffodils are fast beginning, and yesterday in the rectory garden of St. Ervan, near the north coast just beyond Newquay, I saw such a sweet spread of snowdrops, and a fine *Mahonia japonica* with its shining dark green leaves and plenty of deliciously scented lily-of-the-valley-like flowers, in spreading racemes of pale yellow.

Our crocuses too are gay – yellow and purple and white.

> For lo, the winter is past, the rain is over and gone;
> The flowers appear on the earth;
> The time of singing of birds is come.

> (*Song of Songs*, ii, 10–13).

The words apply – except the second half of the first line. That never can be quoted with any certainty in Cornwall.

> (*The Guardian*, 28 March 1947, p. 130.)

Kew in Spring
The Most for a Penny

One penny only is still the charge for admission to the Royal Botanic Gardens at Kew, and the visitor can stay from ten in the morning till seven in the evening, drinking in beauty and peace all the time. He is allowed to wander where he will and the plants are plainly labelled so that he can store his mind with knowledge as well as with delight. This, surely, must be far the best pennyworth in the world.

It has been a late season, after the severest winter within living memory, so that I was not prepared to find the garden so full of life and loveliness as it proved to be on a showery day in the last week of April. The afternoon cleared completely and the sun shone out with warmth and brightness. I entered by the Victoria Gate and was soon faced up by a group of half-a-dozen or more Canadian *Amelanchiers*, their black trunks and branches hidden beneath a cloud of light, white flowers. The path to the right leads to a lake and No.1 Museum. As I turned that way I had on my left a bed of [Peaches], flowering a rich pink on the bare wood. There were about a dozen of them (*Prunus persica*) with a carpet of blue *Anemones* beneath. Under some beeches just bursting into leaf a little further on were low masses of a *Mahonia* with dark green leaves out of which rose rich yellow knobs of tiny blossoms. On the other side of the path the shining gold of taller clumps of *Forsythia* was simply dazzling, and a little past them another variety of *Prunus persica* was a lovely spectacle, with double flowers of deep pink thick along the branches, each of which was tipped with slender leaves of a tender Spring brown. On No.1 Museum itself was a Quince with flowers consisting of carmine-red petals spread round small clusters of yellow stamens.

But on this occasion I did not wish to go further in that direction but to strike out from the Victoria Gate towards the so-called Temple of King William. This little structure, one of several in the Gardens, was built by William IV on a mound about a hundred and fifty yards north of the Temperate House. According to local tradition the workman was cutting the King's initials on the pediment of this temple when the great bell of St. Pauls' began to toll the announcement of his death.

How astonishing is the fresh Spring green on an ancient larch, and what wonderful flowering trees are the *Magnolias*! It is only right that they should be reintroduced into this country. They were here before the Ice-Age, and they soon make themselves thoroughly at home. There is an interesting group of them in this part of the garden, though with one exception, not so spectacular as another group a good deal further to the south-west. The exception is a tall *Magnolia campbellii* with great flower-cups of rich pink high up against the blue sky. This is perhaps the loveliest of all the Magnolias, though there are one or two other species grown in the most favoured Cornish gardens which are thought by some to surpass it. Most of the Magnolias at Kew to which I have referred are varieties of *M.* x *soulangeana*, a Magnolia of garden origin, very reliable and strongly to be recommended for gardens of moderate size. In that other group of Magnolias at Kew to which I have referred is the largest *M.* x *soulangeana* I have ever seen; absolutely smothered with great flower-chalices of pinkish white. Another near it and not quite so large, has flowers whiter and less pink, and in the same group is *M.* 'Lennei' with most attractive large pointed buds of a much darker colour. Not far away another variety of *M.* x *soulangeana* has flowers of a rich deep pink, and near it *M.* x *veitchii* has still larger flowers of pure shining white. *M. denudata* from Central China, large and spreading and now propped up, also has large white chalices of flowers; nor must I forget the charming *M. stellata*, more of a bush than a tree, whose slighter flowers have star like petals.

But I have hastened on too fast. This second group of *Magnolias* is beyond King William's Temple to which I am now directing my footsteps. I am drawn this way because the notice near the Victoria Gate recording the most notable objects of interest in the garden at the moment mentions *Cornus nuttallii* in flower near this Temple. And certainly there they are, several plants, among other Dogwoods of less distinction. The most beautiful of them has a generous display of wide open flowers which have four cream petals striped faintly with red, round a small dark boss as centre.

Before I reach the *Cornus*, however, I must stop to admire a number of other trees and shrubs, now at their very best. *Fothergilla major* is very attractive to-day, with its greenish white brushes of flower and its bright crinkly green leaves, a charming shrub for a small garden. And the Cherries! Kew has a number of very large wild cherries (*Prunus avium*), covered entirely with delicate white blossom. And there are many others, far too numerous to mention – masses of budding or full-open pink and white of various shades and tints, with delicate brownish translucent leaf just beginning to show. I put down several names in my note-book – it is always well to have a note-book ready at Kew. I must only name two here: *P.* 'Hokusai' [formerly *lannesiana* 'Amabilis'], from Japan – amabilis indeed, its pink flush just perfect; and *P. serrulata*, of which an upright variety with light pink flowers raises itself out of a bed of grape hyacinth, *Muscari armeniacum* 'Heavenly Blue' – and an extraordinary rich blue it is, though rather too dark for heaven.

For the rest of my visit I must concentrate on *Rhododendrons*. It is too early in the year to see the Rhododendron Dell, though some early varieties were out, most of them hybrids, pink and dark pink. Outstanding are *R.* 'Mrs. Kingsmill', whose large creamy buds turn white and have a faint delicious scent and *R.* 'Margaret Bean', whose charming trusses of yellowish flowers are fringed with a delicate pink. This latter is named after a daughter of our leading writer on Trees and Shrubs, the William Jackson Bean, who died on Saturday, April 19, this year, at the age of 83. He was associated with the Royal Botanic Gardens for more than sixty years, a man of modesty and solid worth, with an unrivalled knowledge of his subject, and a great gift of apt description.

Not far from King William's Temple is an interesting collection of the smaller and dwarf rhododendrons: among others, *R. polycladum*, lavender blue; and a dear little group of *R. hippophaeioides* with rosettes of purple blue at the top of twiggy branches. Larger Rhododendrons are *R.* 'Cunningham's Sulphur', with flowers of suphur yellow, as its name implies, now at perfection: the purple *R.* 'Emasculum' fully out, and *R.* 'Rosy Bell', a good garden hybrid; both in considerable clumps. A fine spreading specimen of the last is planted by itself with the delicate drooping branches of a variety of *Prunus subhirtella* hanging over it, the little pink flowers of the *Prunus* matching well with the rosy bells of the Rhododendron. Two other famous *Rhododendrons* I was glad to see in flower: *R. augustinii*, a rich dark blue, and *R. davidsonianum*, a light purple. I hope I may be excused for remarking that neither of these were anything like as good as specimens I have seen in Cornwall, and that I was quite shocked to see another distinguished *Rhododendron williamsianum* (so called after one of the greatest gardeners of Cornwall, the late John Charles Williams of Caerhays), represented by a small bush in a cramped and crowded position. But I must admit that as a Cornishman I am somewhat spoiled when it comes to *Rhododendrons*. They love the acid soil and the frequent rains of

Cornwall and thrive luxuriantly. On the other hand Kew forges
ahead of Cornwall in several respects in the later Spring. The
Cherries, for example, are much further on than they are in the far
West. The hotter sunshine which they get in the Eastern counties in
the middle of the day brings them on at a prodigious rate. And
Kew's recovery this year from the bitter winter is quite remarkable.
The losses prove not to be so severe after all. I was pleased, for
instance, to see one of the bigger and hardier Rock roses, *Cistus lau-
rifolius*, though somewhat dishevelled, still very much alive.

If I were a Londoner I should adopt a regular custom of
observing Industrial Sunday, the Sunday before May Day. There are
no more industrious workers (at least in my experience) than gardeners. And on Industrial Sunday I should make a practice of repair-
ing to Kew. I would attend morning service in Kew parish church
and then I would take my sandwiches into the Botanic Gardens and
there spend the afternoon. The service in church I should regard as
the saying of Grace before a feast. It is right to have a longer and
more devout Grace than usual; for the feast is ambrosial.

(*The Guardian*, 9 May 1947, pp. 199, 204.)

Pilgrimage to Bitton

On Whitsunday I was awakened at 6 a.m. by the bells of St. Mary's
Launceston, that beautiful and stately church with amazing carving
on its granite walls. After helping at one early service and celebrating at another, I set out after breakfast to drive to Cheltenham to
preach at the centenary festival of the training colleges of St. Mary
and St. Paul. It was a fine morning and I decided that I would turn
a little aside and call at Bitton on my way. I reached the village,
about five miles from Bristol on the Bath road, early in the afternoon and went into the church. It is a large church, consisting
chiefly of one broad main aisle, very long and difficult to manage
if the congregation insists (as so often a congregation does) on sitting at the back. On the north side of the chancel I read the inscription on the tablet to Canon Ellacombe:

The Lych Gate was erected in memory of Henry
Nicholson Ellacombe, M.A., Oxon., Vicar of this parish

1850–1916, Hon. Canon of Bristol Cathedral, Rural Dean
of Bitton.

Canon Ellacombe was one of the great gardeners of his day.
The 107th volume of the *Botanical Magazine* (1861) was dedicated to
him. No less than nineteen of the plates in that remarkable journal,
which has continued from 1787 down to the present day, were
taken from plants supplied by the canon. For nineteen years he was
connected with *The Guardian*, and I had read the charming gardening articles which he contributed during 1890–1893 and collected in
a volume published under the title *In a Gloucestershire Garden* (1895).
I had also read with great pleasure his later volume, *In my Vicarage
Garden and Elsewhere* (1902), and the Memoir edited by A.W. Hill in
1919. No wonder, then, that I had long been eager to make a pilgrimage to Bitton. The present vicar, the Rev. Lendon Bell, very
kindly gave me permission to look round the garden, and told me
a number of things about the old régime under the canon. The
house is in the middle of a cup among the hills and is rather damp.
In the winter Canon Ellacombe used to have fires lit every day in
bedrooms, as well as sitting-rooms, to the number of nine! And
now the vicar and his family gallantly cope with the house and the
one and a half acres of garden with but a bare minimum of help.
Before I left, the vicar said that there was an old gardener in the village who had worked for the canon, and that if I would call again
some day he would arrange for him to take me round. "No time like
the present", I replied, and arranged to come the next afternoon on
my way back from Cheltenham.

The festival of the colleges was full of enthusiasm and encouragement: Whit Monday was warm and bright, and by 3 p.m. I was
at Bitton again. Mr. Albert Miller, the gardener, was waiting by the
churchyard gate to greet me, a man now in his eighties, still alert and
observant and with a good memory. He had worked for the canon
for twenty years; and his father for thirty-two years before him.

It was indeeed a pleasure to be taken by Mr. Miller on the tour
of the garden in the very order in which the canon himself used to
conduct his visitors. A great many of the canon's plants, of course,
had died, but it was very interesting to see how many had remained
or were still represented by their offspring. It must suffice to mention a few of the most outstanding. A fine big service tree was laden
with white blossom; the great fern-leaved beech, planted before the
canon's time, was beautiful as ever; the tulip tree had suffered in

recent years, and so had the [*Robinia*] *pseudoacacia*, planted on the birth of the canon's son Gilbert; but the gingko, whose autumn colouring he used so much to admire, was still flourishing vigorously. Canon Ellacombe was particularly fond of species roses. He used to say that roses grown as lasting ornaments in the garden can scarcely be too much left to themselves. Among a number that had long been left to themselves I saw the apple rose (a large fruited variety of *R. villosa*), a charming little white Scotch rose, and several thriving plants of *Rosa sericea* f. *pteracantha*, the rose whose principal charm lies in its thorns. They consist of large flat spines through which the light shines bright red. On a wall of the vicarage was a white *Clematis montana* which had been there as long as the gardener could remember, and also a *Magnolia grandiflora* of the superior 'Exmouth' variety. Mr. Miller recalled with evident delight the canon's white fritillaries, the *Iris reticulata* which used to flower when the snow was on the ground, the sweet-scented autumn-flowering cyclamen, and the alliums and the acanthus, of both of which the canon once had a large number of varieties. He chuckled over *Ornithogalum pyrenaicum* (quite a weed, he said, in the garden), whose young shoots used to be sold in the shops as Bath asparagus. He remembered the beautiful black grapes which grew on the screen out of doors, how the canon would bring out bags of nuts for the nuthatches, and how the bees filled with honey a hole made in a tree by a woodpecker. We looked for the old-fashioned *Ranunculus* with its white buttons, for *Lonicera fragrantissima*, the Chinese honeysuckle, the earliest to flower, and the *Lithospermum* carpeting the ground under an English oak. Mr. Miller pointed out a well-grown specimen of that small nut tree with strangely contorted branches – *Corylus avellana* 'Contorta'.

Three of the plants which I had particularly associated with the canon were *Poncirus trifoliata*, *Diospyros kaki* and *Chimonanthus praecox*. I found them all. The first was about twelve feet high. It has not done well so far with me in Cornwall, but in the canon's garden it bore its citron-like fruit freely. The second, the persimmon, also used to bear its handsome and delicious fruit in the canon's time, but since then it had suffered severely and is now barely alive. The third, the wintersweet I was most glad of all to see living still. The canon used often to enclose a bare sprig of it, starred with close-fitting fragrant little flowers, in a winter letter to a friend.

Other plants which I saw were a fine white-flowered quince, a pink bush honeysuckle, a great bed of Spanish gorse recovering from the severity of the last winter, a big Japanese vine, an almost white wisteria, a *Deutzia* with rose-coloured blossoms flowering better (Mr. Miller said) than ever before, a *Viburnum plicatum* f. *tomentosum* 'Mariesii' which the canon used to call his table plant on account of its flat top; a good *Magnolia* x *soulangeana* 'Lennei', with its chalices of dark purple. There were several varieties of berberis, including B. *congestiflora* which a gardener from Kew said it was worth coming all the way from Kew to see. There were also the hydrangea of gaunt habit and with bristly shoots and leaves, *H. sargentiana*, the hardiest of the *Eucryphias* (*E. glutinosa*), and the Dutchman's Pipe, *Aristolochia macrophylla*. Nor must I forget a trellis of *Parthenocissus henryana*, like a very handsome virginia creeper, and the holly called the milkmaid holly on account of its white variegation.

Canon Ellacombe's favourite doctrine was that a true gardener is known by the pleasure he takes in giving plants to his friends. Before they left the garden he would always say, "I hope you have found something to take away with you." *Petimusque damusque vicissim* (We seek and give in turn) was the motto which headed his manuscript garden-book. Accordingly I brought several little flowers and sprigs away with me, including a piece of hedgehog holly, rightly named because of the blobs of prickles on the surface as well as on the edges of the leaves.

Time was for a time forgotten till the vicar brought us a tray of tea upon the lawn. Then very gracefully I said farewell, and drove the straight way home. From time to time I met a little stream of Whit-Monday traffic. Once I stopped for petrol, and once in the middle of Dartmoor for a cup of coffee. The evening sun lit up the valleys winding on to the moor, and then I hastened on through greyness and gathering dusk. But it was hardly dark when at length I drew up at my own door an hour before midnight.

(*The Guardian*, 11 July 1947, p. 310.)

Climbers – Wanted and Unwanted

According to William Robinson, whose *English Flower Garden* is one of the most influential books which have ever been written on gardening, the clematis is the most beautiful of the northern climbing plants, which, rightly grown, are hardy in this country. Certainly,

again and again this summer on my way to the Midlands, I have
seen *Clematis* x *jackmanii* festooning the porch of a cottage with rich
abundance of great flowers of violet-purple, four or five inches
across. Earlier in the year, at the end of May, I saw a lovely *Clematis
montana* var. *rubens* covering with rosy pink blossoms the wall and a
great part of the roof of a cottage in Gloucestershire. There are
hosts of other beauties all related to Old Man's Beard, the only
clematis native of this country. If allowed to grow freely, this is
capable of reaching a height of fifty feet, and the great thongs
forming the base of the twining growths will be as thick as a man's
arm. Its masses of attractive whitish flowers are succeeded by heads
of silvery, silky seed which will remain into the winter, long after all
the leaves have fallen. The other name of this familiar climber tes-
tifies to its popularity – The Traveller's Joy.

But what shall we say about ivy, the common ivy? I have just
received peremptory warning from the diocesan surveyor against
allowing the ivy to cover the outside of my garden wall. Many people think that serious damage is done to trees by allowing ivy to
climb over them. There is good reason, however, to suppose that as
long as the ivy is confined to the trunk and larger branches no harm
is done. There are trees still in perfect health which have supported
ivy for forty years. As far as buildings are concerned, I am afraid the
overwhelming opinion of architects is against the ivy. Honesty
compels me to admit it. But I shall not forget a Sunday morning in
the middle of last October, when I saw a mass of ivy covering two
sides of the tower of Landewednack church, near the Lizard,
smothered with rich umbels of yellow flowers. The ivy sprang from
a great trunk-like stem, and its trim spread was really magnificent.

When I reported this beautiful intruder to one of the most
distinguished of our Cornish gardeners, he looked at me with dis-
appoval, and said, "But why not the climbing hydrangea?" Why not
indeed? It has pleasant green leaves and, in June, plentiful flat
corymbs of tiny florets with larger white flowers on the margins. In
the well-kept garden of Trelawne, near Looe, the ancestral home of
the Trelawny family, now a hostel for retired clergy and their wives,
there is a tall fir tree, whose bare trunk is elegantly clothed, right up
to the scanty leafy branches at its head, with the slender twining
branches of a healthy and floriferous climbing hydrangea. Another
striking sight in the same garden last year was a mass of the Chilean
nasturtium (*Tropaeolum speciosum*) growing over a tall clipped hedge
of *Cupressus macrocarpa*. Its numberless little flowers of vermillion

red stood out charmingly upon the background of fresh green. Canon Gotto has had a fine display of the same nasturtium in his vicarage garden at Porthleven; and I am trying it here at Lis Escop, Truro, though, so far, with no great success. A well-established climbing hydrangea, however, against a wall of Lis Escop chapel, has been finer this year than ever before. Near it, on the north wall of the chapel, is one of the choice plants of the garden, *Lapageria rosea*, given me years ago by the late Canon Arthur Boscawen, V.M.H., whose rectory garden at Ludgvan must have been in many ways the finest in England. Canon Bosacawen very kindly came and planted it with his own hands. It is the national flower of Chile, and its long pendulous tubes of crimson have upon their surface a fine shining granulation which makes them appear to be made of frozen snow. My plant has flourished wonderfully, though the late winter hit it hard. It is coming on again, but there will be no flowers this year.

From further south in South America I have Lord Anson's pea (*Lathyrus nervosus*). Lord Anson, commanding H.M.S. *Centurion* in 1744, sent ashore for vegetables, and the cook saved some of these peas and introduced the plant to England. The flowers are a beautiful blue, dark, almost to Oxford blue, when it lives frugally on poor soil (compare the two Universities).

From Chile again I have that bright and charming little shrub, introduced by a Cornishman, William Lobb, about a hundred years ago, *Mitraria coccinea*. Its scarlet tubular flowers, with yellow anthers protruding beyond the corolla, are very attractive. My plant has already displayed its climbing propensities, and though it suffered a good deal last winter it had made some recovery. At Kew it requires greenhouse treatment.

Somewhat hardier is the Passion-flower from South Brazil. Mine is on a south wall, as it should be; but for some time I was afraid that the frost last winter had killed it. It did nothing of the sort, I am glad to say, and the spreading branches are now covered with large buds. The name is due to the Spanish priests who detected in the flower symbols of the instruments of the Passion: the three stigmas representing the three nails; the five anthers the five wounds; the corona the crown of thorns; the five sepals and five petals the ten apostles (Peter and Judas being absent); the hand-like leaves, the hands, and the whip-like tendrils the scourges of Christ's tormentors.

Another Brazilian climber which makes a beautiful display on cottage walls in the south-west of England is the Jasmine-like

Solanum (*Solanum jasminoides*). It produces its greyish blue flowers in great profusion. Jasmines, honeysuckles, and rambler roses I must here omit. There are so many of them. They are sweet and familiar as their names. My strongest-growing honeysuckle, outside my study window, needs a curb, or it will stangle its neighbour. It was given me by the late Mr. John Charles Williams, of Caerhays. For some years it hardly flowered, but, coming from Mr. Williams I knew it must be good, and now it floods the near part of the garden with sweetness – not quite the usual honeysuckle scent but something between that and the scent of the philadelphus (commonly, but incorrectly, called syringa).

The neighbour is a Chinese shrub with dark glossy green leaves and unfortunately no popular name, but only a long technical one: *Trachelospermum jasminoides*. I did not realize that it was a climber until three or four years ago when it began sending out long slender twining shoots up my study wall. Its white jasmine-like flowers are delightfully fragrant. It, too, was hit last winter, but now seems to be very little the worse. It goes on flowering from July to September.

Further east, at a corner of the house, another Chinese climber has begun to do well, *Schisandra chinensis*. It has pretty rose-coloured flowers on slender stalks, and they should be succeeded by scarlet berries, which remain on the plant during the winter. I have just been to try to find some of these berries forming. I could see none, but the plant was plainly being overwhelmed by the Virgina creeper coming round from the other side of the house. Not that I should wish to include Virgina creeper in a list of the unwanted, but its greediness must receive a decisive check. In point of fact it has also been intruding on my wisterias on the front of the house, and particularly on the younger and more fragrant, the white one. Their flowering period is in May and June, but, looking out of my bedroom window last evening, I saw one single drooping raceme of the pale mauve flowers just appearing, and I have since counted four more.

Near the wisterias I have set two little plants of *Akebia quinata*, a twining shrub also from the Far East. They were given me by Mrs. Charles Doughty, the widow of the author of *Arabia Deserta*, one of the great travel books of the world. Mrs Doughty has settled at Falmouth with her two daughters, and though eighty-five still works hard in her beautiful garden. I saw the slender pendant racemes of fragrant pale purple flowers on an akebia climbing up her house. Mrs. Douglty told me that she always planted one wherever she went, and very kindly offered me a couple of young seedlings. I gratefully accepted them, and they have made a good start, though I must not expect them to flower just yet.

They are actually replacing another unusual climber, *Ipomoea lobata*, from Australia. The seed of this was sent to me from Sydney, and when a young Australian flying-officer came to stay with us for a short leave during the war he was very pleased to find such a reminder of home. It has deeply-lobed leaves and an abundance of small bright red and yellow pea-like flowers. I am sorry we have lost it. We must try to get some more seed.

Similarly we must make another attempt with the lobster claw (*Clianthus puniceus*), also called the parrot's bill, from New Zealand. On a south wall some years ago it gave us masses of its brilliant crowded lobster claws; and two years ago I had a most promising plant growing vigorously up the wall at the back of my study fire. It evidently revelled in the transmitted heat. But one week during the winter when I was away in London and the study fire was not lit the weather turned sharp, and the plant immediately died.

I pass on now to a climber most certainly unwanted in a garden: *Convolvulus*, the bindweed. Its twining stems, its fresh shapely leaves and white flowers, are in themselves attractive enough. But the convolvulus won't keep itself to itself. It must needs straddle over everything. My raspberries would have disappeared under the smother of it, if it had not been for my meticulous belated efforts. Happily the bindweeds have more manageable relatives, and one of the most delightful shall bring up the rear of this little parade: *C. sebatius*. I brought it back from the great garden at Tresco in the Isles of Scilly, and it is now very happy, forming prostrate clumps in a sunny corner. It shuts its flower-funnels tightly each evening, and opens them wide and smiling in the sun, and their colour is the loveliest soft violet-purple I have ever seen.

(*The Guardian*, 5 September 1947, p. 406.)

Recovery

No place in the British Isles enjoys a more equable climate than the Isles of Scilly. Even the rigours of last winter reached the Isles in a very moderated and mitigated form. Nevertheless those rigours were so unusual, and for the Isles so severe, that the effect to the great garden at Tresco was at first sight devastating. The lowest temperature reached was but 8 degrees below freezing point, though the thermometer stood just below freezing point for several days, and the snow lay on the ground to a depth of nine inches or more for five days.

The hard winter was succeeded by a wet spring and early summer and then by a fine dry August. I found it very interesting to go round the garden in September and see what the position was by that time to compare losses and recoveries with those in my own garden at Lis Escop, Truro. Here, on four separate occasions, we registered 18 degrees of frost, and the subsequent rains were heavy and continuous over a long period.

Among the most notable features of Tresco are the fine Iron-trees from New Zealand, some of them a hundred years old. In July they should be smothered in bright red blossoms blazing far out to sea: but not this year. They are very susceptible to damage by frost, and for that reason do not succeed on the mainland, even in Cornwall. Last winter left most of the trees in Scilly apparently dead: but not quite all. The worst were in what must have been frost-pockets, though they looked like comparatively sheltered positions. Here and there, notably in the little churchyard facing north-east and on a tiny island in the middle of the freshwater lake below the Abbey House, a more exposed tree came through the ordeal only slightly scorched. And now all the Iron-trees show curious signs of life. Amid a great deal of dead wood, and along the trunks and branches, tiny shoots bearing little leaves of shining green have appeared in hundreds. Before long they will make new branches, crowding one another to such an extent that only the most favourably placed will ultimately survive. In the course of time the dead wood will be broken off by the wind, and the trees will be bright and red again in July and well-furnished with dark green leaves throughout the year. These leaves have a white tomentum underneath: hence the name of the tree – *Metrosideros excelsa.*[1]

When the frosts came last January the garden at Tresco was gay with the red spikes of many aloes. These speedily perished, and many of their fleshy stems still present a picture of decay. But let them alone. There is life yet in some of the rosettes of succulent green leaves at the tops of the stems, and they will send down fresh roots which will eventually reach the ground even through the old decayed stems. The aloes are mostly African. Their near relatives,

the agaves from America, have fared much better, and the biggest
of them, with their fierce spikes on their huge, thick, smooth, succulent grey leaves, look more impressive than ever, standing out
above the Middle Terrace. One, below the Abbey house, is actually
in flower, and its tall mast with yellow flowers clustered at the end
of short branches is singular and striking.

Also in full bloom when the frosts came were the great tender-
looking clumps of *Sparmannia africana*. Their white flowers with
golden stamens are often seen in greenhouses. In the open at
Tresco the shrubs flourish luxuriantly, but last January they were
grievously smitten. Now, drastically cut back, and mere shadows of
their former selves, they are breaking into leaf again.

The Australian correas were also to some extent in flower.
Tresco has several beautiful kinds with pink and white or greenish,
fuchsia-like tubes of flower. None of them were seriously harmed. I
had a small bed of them at Truro and all were killed. I had another
promising little Australian *Bursaria spinosa*, the Tasmanian Christmas
Tree. That, too, was killed; but a much larger one at Tresco was
smothered with delicate white flower again this summer. Similarly
all my lovely dark blue *Hebes* were left stone dead, but at Tresco they
escaped. One *Hebe* only survived with me, *H. buxifolia*, very hardy
and floriferous. This year its cheerful spikes of small white flowers
have been gayer than usual. At Tresco both the common myrtle and
Luma apiculata, a myrtle from Chile, have flowered more freely than
ever. Their little white blossoms are succeeded by black berries. The
escallonias also have been excellent. The white alder trees (*Clethra
arborea*) from Madeira, on the other hand, have produced fewer than
usual of their racemes of fragrant lily-of-the-valley flowers this
August.

Of the numerous acacias only one or two species have been
seriously hurt, and of the brooms only one, the white one from
North Africa. The great Canary Island palms stand up stately as
ever, though some of their huge fronds are scorched brown. The
tall cordylines (better known as dracaena – there is a road in
Falmouth lined with them and called Dracaena Avenue) look a bit
dishevelled, and so do the big Fan-palms (*Trachycarpus*), though the
lower ones appear untouched. The Nikau palm [*Rhopalostylis sapida*],
whatever its inner condition may be, is flowering again. Its singular
rod of pink flowers is perched oddly on the side of its great thick
smooth trunk of shiny green. The banksias, the Australian honeysuckle trees, seem little hurt. There has been a great mortality

among the hakeas, but the delicate white brushes of flowers have appeared on the top of the white-mantled tea tree (*Melaleuca linarifolia*). The New Zealand daisy-bushes (*Olearias*) are all right; and the attractive ever-green pittosporums have not been seriously affected. Most of mine at Lis Escop have come through their ordeal too. It is otherwise with my starry-flowered leptospermums. They have been decimated, but the leptospermums at Tresco are still in good shape. *Senna corymbosa* at Tresco is covered with its blossoms of rich yellow, which, with the paler yellow of an acacia, helped to adorn the harvest thanksgiving in the little church of St Nicholas. My plant, though in the most sheltered position I could give it, perished utterly.

The rock-roses in both places have stood the trial well. I was particularly glad to see a big clump of the large-leaved one, *Cistus populifolius*. Their leaves give forth such a rich aromatic fragrance which, together with that of the various species of Australian gum-trees (*Eucalyptus*), I always associate with the Tresco garden. Most of the euclyptuses at Tresco seem hardly touched. One or two with me were killed, but they were not sufficiently established to stand much chance.

The furcraeas at Tresco came through the winter well, and one of the smaller plants produced its tall mast of flower. Similarly that strange stiff desert plant from Mexico with spiny margined leaves, the dasylirion, is flourishing as ever, and is now adorned with a high spike of greenish flowers which I have never seen before. This particular example has the strangest kink half-way up, owing to the action of the wind.

The griselinias are untouched, both the ordinary one which we have in Cornwall and the large-leaved one, thought to be more tender. *Calceolaria integrifolia* is still producing its yellow flowers in the garden of Tresco parsonage, and a thicket of *Jovellana violacea* in the Abbey garden is unharmed. The great leaves of *Brachyglottis repanda* are plentiful, though the small trees have certainly suffered. The undersides of the leaves are so white that it is quite easy to write a letter on them. *Echiums* are very plentiful in the garden. The bush echiums have suffered severely, but the single stemmed ones seem little the worse, and several of them are still showing their pole-like spike of numerous tiny flowers.

Perhaps the two most notable Tresco casualties are the karaka [*Corynocarpus laevigata*] and the puka [*Meryta sinclairii*], both from New Zealand. The former in its native home is a coastal plant. Its large seeds, poisonous when fresh, after being washed and dried are eaten by the Maoris and much esteemed. The latter, with its immense leaves of lustrous green is rare, and come from the Hen and Chickens and the Three Kings Islands off the coast of New Zealand. It will bear strong winds but not frost. Happily one or two of its seedlings have survived. And that illustrates the fact, noticeable both at Scilly and on the mainland, that some of the younger and smaller plants have come through the winter better than some of the older and larger. This is partly due to their having received more protection from the heavy fall of the snow.

Both at Scilly and in Cornwall the fate of some plants is still in the balance. Earlier in the summer they showed some small hopeful shoots springing generally from low down; but now they look sickly and seem hardly able to maintain their convalescence. The only thing to do is to wait and see.

But I can end this brief account on a more cheerful note. Some of the gayest and most charming things at Tresco are the low things on the ground. Many of them are tender enough, but their roots were covered by the snow and though in February they looked dead, they have grown green again and even spread under the earth. I refer specially to the pelargoniums, commonly called geraniums. For many years Tresco has had masses of them. The old garden list contains the names of over a hundred and fifty varieties. The maintenance of these delightful groups with flowers of bright colours and deliciously scented leaves has been skilfully managed by the head gardener Mr. W.G. Andrews, who keeps on striking cuttings and replenishes any varieties which show a tendency to decrease. After the great frost a good number of varieties recovered on their own account, but some did not. Mr. Andrews has been able to replace most of the losses, but there are still one or two gaps. For example, if any gardener could send him a few cuttings of 'Rollinson's Unique' he would be very grateful. Last year I brought home from Scilly cuttings of 'Pretty Polly', pink and white, and 'Moore's Victory', a most attractive dark scarlet. They were struck under glass and this summer planted out in large pots on the terrace in good time for the archbishop's visit on the occasion of the diamond jubilee of Truro Cathedral (July 20).

Mesembryanthemums at Scilly fared like the pelargoniums. They also number over a hundred and fifty in the garden list, and they provide similar patches of ever more brilliant colour: yellows, oranges, purples, whites and reds. Such a display no place on the mainland can rival. "Mesmerisms", as Mr. Augustus Smith, the creator of the Tresco garden used to call them, have been in the garden for over a hundred years, but their succulent stems and leaves look far too vulnerable for me to invite them to Lis Escop. Some in exposed positions at Tresco were killed by the frost: *Lampranthus blandus* and *productum* (both pale rose) for example. But many survived, and the losses are being rapidly replaced; and already the garden is lit up with a number of the accustomed patches of brilliance.

When I had finished my tour, on the way to the shore, I came upon an unexpected example, not so much of recovery as of complete escape. In a corner by an out-house behind a cottage there was a fine aloe with its green rosettes of leaves quite untouched, and behind and above it a tall pelargonium topped triumphantly by flowers of a delicate and beautiful scarlet.

(*The Guardian*, 7 November 1947, pp. 514–15.)

1 Formerly *tomentosa*. *Metrosideros* in Greek literally means 'heart-wood of iron', but they are more usually referred to by their New Zealand names, which are:- *M. robusta* the 'Northern Rata', *M. umbellata* the 'Southern Rata', and *M. excelsa* the 'Christmas Tree' or 'Pohutukawa'. These three and six other species have been grown on Tresco. See page 92 for the trees more usually described as 'ironwood'.

A Hundred Years or More

In a subdued frame of mind after a cordial but slow-creeping conference with charming and distinguished Lutherans, I drove one day last October into the middle of the lovely county of Sussex to spend the weekend with a friend. In my bedroom to welcome me he had placed a vase of *Zauschneria* [now *Epilobium*], the California fuschia. I was delighted with its little ash-grey leaves and sprays of scarlet tubular flowers. I did not know till I looked it up that it was named in honour of Dr. Zauschner, a Professor at Prague, who died in 1799, and that this is the centenary year of its introduction into this country. Other beautiful plants celebrating their centenary this year are *Ceanothus rigidus* from South California, and two lovelies from Chile, *Philesia* and *Lapageria*. The ceanothus has been consid-

ered one of the more tender of its family, but it seems to be prov-
ing itself hardier than was supposed, and its bright blue flowers are
very attractive.

Philesia has crisp dark green foliage and rosy crimson flowers.
Plants in Cornwall survived the unusually severe frost of last winter. So did *Lapageria rosea* on the north wall of the chapel of the
Bishop's house (Lis Escop) at Truro. It was given to me a few years
ago by that great green-fingered gardener, the late Canon Arthur
Boscawen. He chose the place and planted the lapageria with his
own hands. It is the national flower of Chile, and its long bells of
deep pink have a frosty granulation upon their surface, so that they
appear to be made of richly coloured snow. It suffered severely last
winter, but it has survived and has gallantly borne two great flowers, one of which is depending from it still.

A hundred years ago, then; there was considerable activity in
introducing exotic plants into Great Britain: and so there was long
before that. My attention has just been drawn to a manuscript in the
library of Magdalen College, Oxford, published in the *Gardeners'
Chronicle* (May, 1920), which contains Latin lists of plants grown
three hundred years ago at Darfield Rectory in the West Riding of
Yorkshire. The rector, the Rev. Walter Stonehouse, formerly a
Fellow of Magdalen, was instituted in 1631 and ejected by the
Parliamentary Committee and imprisoned. He died in 1655 at the
age of fifty-eight. His lists include fourteen plants from Virginia,
five from Guinea, and four from New England. From 1640 to 1644
he counted altogether 866 species in his garden. Many of the names
are familiar enough: anemone, aquilegia, campanula, colchicum,
crocus, fritillary, gladiolus, hollyhock, iris, narcissus, paeony, rose-
mary, with roses and tulips of many kinds.

The manuscript contains plans of the rectory grounds. There
was "the best garden", 34 yards by 30 yards, laid out formally in five
"knots" in sixteenth-century style. There were also an orchard and
a "saffron garth", both walled. On the walls fruit trees were trained:
plums, peaches, apricots and pomegranates. There was also a vine,
perhaps on the wall of the rectory itself.

Among the apples there are a number of old names: Kentish
codling, golden pippin, gilloflower, leathercoat (a dessert russet);
and the John Apple and Flower of Kent, both good cookers.

"The saffron garth nine times round", the rector says, "wants
fifty yards of a mile." Here he grew crocuses, presumably for the
production of saffron. Cornishmen have a special interest in saf-

fron. Well I remember as a boy looking forward to the baking of saffron cakes and buns, plentifully sprinkled with currants, every fortnight at home. The saffron used for colouring and flavouring consists of the stigmas of *Crocus sativus*. "Our English honey and saffron", says a writer in 1588, "is better than any that cometh from any strange or foreign land." In those days saffron was sold at £1 a pound, a pound sterling of course being worth vastly more than it is to-day. But the price was not excessive considering that it takes 4,320 flowers to produce one ounce of saffron. The main crop came from the district of Saffron Walden (hence the name), and it is rather surprising to find the cultivation so far north as Yorkshire. But Darfield Rectory has in recent times been noted for a crocus border 170 yards long.

Stonehouse was a careful observer and a good scholar. He was one of the first Englishmen to make a collection of coins and medals. His manuscript ends with some Latin verses as the epitaph of Delia, a favourite cat, buried in the garden. What a shame to drag so gentle a gardener away to prison! In 1652 he returned, and to his total of 866 plants he added a Latin note: "of which to-day few, alas, remain, *novamque despero coloniam* – and I have no hope of founding another colony." What a naughty world it was – and is!

(*The Guardian*, 24 December 1947, p. 596.)

The Glass of Fashion

In the various departments of the General Store of human activity the changes of fashion make an interesting study. The gardening department affords a good example.

If we take as our starting point the year 1066 – the starting point for so many things – we find the peaceful act of gardening practised most effectively at that unsettled time in the monasteries, especially, perhaps by the Benedictines who aimed at being self-supporting. The earliest surviving plan of a monastic garden in England appears to be that in a Canterbury manuscript of about 1165 now in the library of Trinity College, Cambridge. This shows the herbarium between the dormitory and the infirmary, surrounded by cloisters, and, also the orchard and vineyard which were situated beyond the walls of the monastery.

It is not generally realized that British climate in the Dark Ages was a good deal worse than it is now, and that a distinct change for the better occurred about the time of the Norman Conquest. Most of the monasteries owned vineyards, and "the wine-making tradition, inherited from Europe, died hard." I take this quotation from a very interesting book just published by the honorary secretary of the Institute of Landscape Architects, Brenda Colvin, under the title *Land and Landscape*, to which I am indebted for much of the information contained in the following paragraphs. The herbarium, i.e., the herb-garden, of the monastery or manor house, contained not only herbs and vegetables but also roses and other scented flowers. The fishponds led before long to pools of more ornamental design; and the use of the garden as a place of refreshment, as well as an adjunct to the kitchen, steadily grew as the country became more settled. "By Tudor times the garden had spread beyond the protecting wall and moat ... and lawns, alleys and flower gardens were lavishly laid out." A good idea of an Elizabethan "Knot-garden", with beds often arranged in groups of geometrical knots, is given by the gay plot on the site of Shakespeare's house at Stratford-on-Avon. These Knot-gardens were regarded as over-elaborate by Francis Bacon in his celebrated essay *Of Gardens*, where he speaks of them as "but Toys, you may see as good sights many times in Tarts." Bacon, indeed, is the prophet of a new style of gardening. He disapproved of topiary work in gardens, with shrubs trimmed to sculptural shapes. "I for my part do not like Images cut out in Juniper and other garden stuff; they are for Children." He favoured the large garden with green lawn and a "wilderness", and he gives much wise advice as to the provision of shelter from the wind and the value of sun and shade. But topiary work still flourished, and Bacon's reaction against formality in garden design seems to have had very little influence at the time. Not only did hounds and horses continue to be cut out in box, but we hear of the Sermon on the Mount with Christ and the multitude in yew.

John Milton may have had Bacon's ideas in mind when he described the lay-out of Paradise, not as that of a formal garden, but as a "wilderness" with thickets, and overhead

> Insuperable height of loftiest shade,
> Cedar and Pine and Fir and branching Palm,
> A sylvan scene ...

With

> Flowers worthy of Paradise, which not nice art
> In beds and curious knots, but Nature boon
> Poured forth profuse on Hill and Dale and Plain.

It was not, however, till the eighteenth century that the landscape garden came into vogue. Joseph Addison and Pope both tilt at the formal garden, and their ideas were put into practice by the famous landscape gardeners, William Kent, Lancelot Brown, Humphry Repton, and their followers. The work of William Kent may be studied at Stowe, where, as Horace Walpole has put it, "he was the first to leap the fence and show that the whole of nature is a garden." The first "ha-ha", or sunken fence, had appeared at Stowe a few years earlier. Its purpose was, of course, to conceal the boundary and open up the view beyond.

Lancelot Brown began as a kitchen-gardener at Stowe and became the most influential landscape gardener of his time. He is supposed to have destroyed more of the older gardens than anyone else. From his habit of saying of any place he was asked to lay out that it had "great capabilities" he became known as "Capability Brown", and someone once said to him; "I hope I may die before you, so that I may see Heaven before you improve it."

Among the extravagances introduced into this type of gardening were dead trees placed by Kent in a London park (laughed at and removed), and even a man hired to sit like a hermit by an artificial cave.

The inevitable reaction began with Repton, who at least allowed a level terrace in front of the house, such as can be seen in the picture of the garden of the poet William Shenstone, where every other hint of formality is avoided. Repton also allowed a "utility" garden to be made on one side of the house, while the picturesque garden remained on the other. Thus use and beauty, which at this period were combined in agriculture, were divorced in gardens.

The next development may be summed up in the word "enrichment." The landscape garden of the eighteenth century had been limited in colour effects to greens and browns and greys, and bright flowers had been largely relegated to the greenhouses. Now, with shrubs as shelter and background, flower-beds were carved out of lawns and filled with scarlet geraniums, yellow calceolarias, and deep-blue lobelias. Twisting paths, winding through shrubberies and doubling back on their tracks, made the garden seem larger than it really was. Foreign conifers were in great favour, on account of their exotic appearance; and the opinion was expressed that no gentleman's place was complete without the Monkey-puzzle (*Araucaria*). The heavy furniture of the nineteenth century and all the knick-knacks crowding the rooms found their counter-parts in the garden. Topiary was revived on a large scale, and flower-beds were constructed in the shape of clocks and baskets.

Against this craze for clipping and carpet-bedding a very effec-tive protest was made by William Robinson, the most influential gardener of modern times. Nature was to be the model again, but Nature in her flowering mood. Flowers, indeed, were to be the main theme, and all else is setting.

Two camps now appeared: Robinson's advocating the informal garden, with his text in the preface to his popular book, *The English Flower Garden*; and the school of formal garden-design, represented by Sir Reginald Blomfield's *Formal Gardens in England*. Miss Gertrude Jekyll, by her planting work, and in her books, showed that a bridge could be built between the two schools; and it is on that bridge that the modern gardener now takes his stand. The pure Architect's garden is too sculptural: the pure Gardener's garden is "a collection of interesting plants, lacking the simplicity of good design." Why should we not have both: beautiful design and plants together? An example leaps to my mind: Mr. George Johnstone's garden at Trewithen, near Grampound Road in Cornwall. There, lovely flowering shrubs and trees are grouped around a long curv-ing lawn in a manner altogether satisfying.

Miss Gertrude Jekyll was not only a distinguished gardener, whose "Notes from Garden and Woodland", contributed to *The Guardian* in 1896 and 1897, were afterwards republished in the most charming of her books, *Wood and Garden*; but she was also a devout Christian, and this article may fittingly conclude with some words from the *Epilogue* to her book, *A Gardener's Testament*, published in 1937, after her death:

> "It must have been at about seven years of age that I first
> learnt to know and love a primrose copse. Since then
> more than half a century has passed, and yet each spring,
> when I wander into the Primrose Wood, and see the pale
> yellow blooms, and smell their sweetest of sweet scents,
> and feel the warm spring air throbbing with the quicken-

ing pulse of new life, and hear the glad notes of the birds
and the burden of the bees, and see again the same delicate young growths piercing the mossy woodland carpet:
when I see and feel and hear all this, for a moment I am
seven years old again and wandering in the fragrant wood
hand-in-hand with the dear God who made it, and who
made the child's mind to open wide and receive the endur-
ing happiness of the gracious gift. So, as by direct divine
teaching, the impression of the simple sweetness of the
Primrose Wood sank deep into the childish heart, and laid
as it were, a foundation stone of immutable belief, that a
Father in Heaven who could make all this, could make
even better if he would, when the time should come that
his children should be gathered about him.

"And as the quick years pass and the body grows old
around the still young heart, and the day of death grows
ever nearer; with each new springtide the sweet flowers
come forth and bloom afresh; and with their coming –
with the ever-renewing of their gracious gift and still more
precious promise – the thought of Death becomes like
that of a gentle and kindly bearer of tidings, who brings
the inevitable message, and bids the one for whom it is
destined receive it manfully and be of good hope and
cheerfulness, and remember that the Sender of Death is
the Giver of the greater new Life, no less that of the
sweet spring flowers that bloom and die and live again as a
never-ending parable of Life and Death and Immortality."

(*The Guardian*, 16 April 1948, p. 184.)

Foretaste of Summer

A day in the garden with no more than two or three telephone calls
– such was Whit Monday. And what a day – a little cloudy to begin
with, and calm: a warm Easterly wind blowing up later on and dying
down again; and the sunshine bright and hot as in summer!

The most arresting sight in the garden is a great clump of
Mollis Azaleas. There are a number of plants of various sizes in the

bed and the colour sequence changes. First came the pinks, and now for a week or two we have been having a perfect blend of gorgeous crimson, flame and yellow. The large clusters of flowers have a sweet honeysuckle scent: so there is nothing lacking to fulfil their joy. Many other scents are now in the garden. Climbing up the front of the house are two wisterias: one large and ancient, reaching to the top of the bell turret, festooned with the familiar drooping racemes of lilac flowers, faintly perfumed: the other, a young plant which I put in three or four years ago at the other end of the façade to train to meet the older one, with shorter racemes of white flowers, similarly, but more decidedly, fragrant. Another lilac-blue wisteria in a different part of the garden has just swung a slender tendril to lay hold upon a walnut tree, and before very long I hope the tree will be swathed with wisteria instead of ivy.

A fine thick clump of the Jerusalem Sage [*Phlomis fruticosa*] upon the terrace in front of the house is just opening dense clusters of bright yellow flowers above its grey-green leaves. I admired this sage first in the Botanic Garden at Oxford some years ago, though I must admit that my own flowers have not turned out to be as fragrant as I expected. A bush of white-flowered choisya, the Mexican orange blossom, exhales a perfume of a rather different kind. The scent of the magnolias is more aromatic. I have two young trees of *M. wilsonii*. Their lovely white saucers of flower, pink within, look down towards the ground and have a distinct and delicious fragrance. *M. wiesneri*, with a wide-spreading habit, has the most scent of all. It is indeed prodigious. My own plant is, as yet, too young to flower.

Very sweetly-scented are the small buttons of bright yellow stamens among the shining green leaves of *Azara dentata* from Chile. Another azara, a slender tree, was well furnished a few weeks ago with much tinier yellow flowers, which filled the air around with the pleasant fragrance of vanilla.

But the most alluring of all the perfumes of the garden in May is that of the rhododendron, 'Lady Alice Fitzwilliam' – a kind of celestial nutmeg. 'Lady Alice Fitzwilliam' is a slight creature, and flowers herself almost to death. Her large buds, flushed with pink, open to white wells of fragrance. I think of all the rhododendrons she is my favourite. Far larger, and immensely distinguished, is *R. falconeri*, with its enormous leaves dark green above and covered with a warm reddish-brown tomentum underneath. Its great fat buds are just opening into rich trusses of white blossom. A good many rhododendrons are getting over: 'Fusilier', for example, of the richest red; and 'Pink Pen' from Pendarves, near Camborne, a superior version of 'Pink Pearl', being of a still fresher and more delightful pink. Masses of the commonest and hardiest of rhododendrons, *R. ponticum*, are now opening their plentiful trusses of purple flowers along the railway line west of Liskeard. It is too much of a gate-crasher to be encouraged in a garden, but another rhododendron very like it ('Fastuosum Flore Pleno') of a better and more lilac purple with frilled corollas, is welcome to a good position on the drive.

A rarity is of interest, especially when it is itself beautiful and desirable. Such is *Vallea stipularis*. I saw it first in the Temperate House at Kew, with charming drooping racemes of little pink and white blossoms, and foliage of light green. My young plant survived the last winter's frost out-of-doors (with some protection). It is in a sheltered corner on a border lined with Mrs Sinkins pinks, common indeed, but ever cheerful and sweet and reliable. Common enough also is the thrift, or sea-pink. But we have a special variety with flower buttons of a darker pink than usual. It was given me by that accomplished gardener, the Rev. C.T. Rowlands. When Vicar of Egloshayle he brought it on in his garden and distributed it to his parishioners: so that you can see it brightening many garden borders in the neighbourhood of Wadebridge.

Something also of a speciality is a hybrid olearia which I brought back from Tresco; *O.* x *scilloniensis* it has been called. It seems to be a hybrid from *O. phlogopappa* but much more completely smothered with its shining little white daisies. Far more sparse are the much larger white flowers lighting up the dark green foliage of the medlar. It is an ancient and shapely tree, well placed in the middle of what we call the "far garden." It bears a good crop of its brown fruit year by year. The medlar belongs to the great natural order of the Rosaceae. We have a circular rose garden, but it is only a moderate success. *Rosa xanthina* f. *spontanea* from North China is not there, but just outside the dining room. Here it is just showing its fragrant buttercup-yellow single flowers in the full sunshine. It did not turn a hair in the severe frosts of the last two winters.

On the other hand the leptospermums from New Zealand, a charming feature of many Cornish gardens, were, most of them, killed or nearly killed. Two of mine just survived: one, with a profusion of little white starry flowers, is an old inhabitant in the garden; the other had to have its main trunk cut right down, but from a minor limb is growing again and showing numerous buds of blush pink.

The cistus also suffered severely, but a hardy one with wide saucers of purple is now blossoming freely. The tree paeonies seem remarkably hardy, and the best one I have has a lovely single white flower with gold stamens and a slight pleasant perfume. I am not very partial to weigela, still less, as a rule, to variegation of foliage. But this year a very pretty pink and white weigela has so matched her blossoms to her variegated leaf that I relent.

The wild part of the garden is light woodland, all red and blue with campion and bluebells, and patches of the pencilled geranium, the white flowers of which have blue stamens and a delicate light purple veining. Here and there also are tall self-sown brooms forming short wind-screen hedges ablaze with yellow; and, of still brighter yellow, are the prickly round mounds of spanish gorse.

Among all these cheerful friends I spent my Bank Holiday in great content: cutting out dead wood from the shrubs, checking the upstart bindweed among the raspberry canes, nipping off the heads of the penstemons to make them bush out, and starting a hopeless campaign against the great army of plantains which have almost captured the lawn. Inspired by the foretaste of warmth and sunshine I also set forward preparations for our full summer display; and especially for my favourite item – large brown pots along the terrace, containing scented-leaf pelargoniums. My two are 'Pretty Polly', pink and white; and 'Moore's Victory', a rich scarlet with black markings.

(*The Guardian*, 11 June 1948, p. 280.)

Whole Holiday

We were halfway through the long Conference at Lambeth. Our headmaster, the Archbishop of Canterbury, had kept us hard at work: morning, afternoon, and even after tea: and the week-end break was very welcome. The headlines in the Press that Saturday morning had announced the arrival of sixty Superfortresses from the United States of America – "Superforts fly in." So it was somewhat weary and disturbed that I approached the Victoria Gate of the Royal Gardens at Kew. It was a fine morning. Not many people were about, and a few steps inside the gate peace descended upon

me. I breathed the soothing sweet scent of the lime, and there burst
upon me the astonishing hope of the fresh tufts of bright green at
the end of the branches of the Bhutan pine [*P. wallichiana*]. I passed
a sweet chestnut heavily in flower – as it was in my own Cornish
garden too. The flowers have a peculiar smell, slightly like that of
elder and not very pleasant; and I was glad to leave it behind and to
enjoy the aromatic scent exhaled from the leaves of the gum cistus
as I went by a large bed of it. Most of the flowers were over, but
there were still some gay survivors, all wide open, with bright yellow stamens, some with petals of light purple. I was walking in the
direction of the Temperate House. Near that great structure,
severely damaged in the war but now repaired, I saw a shapely
Indian Bean [*Catalpa bignonioides*], with a spreading head of large
glaucous fresh-green leaves. It was about to flower. The Indian
Beans in Parliament Yard, Westminster, are still finer, and their
white panicles flower abundantly. I was admiring these Parliament
trees, one morning with a young policeman, and he told me that the
finest specimen in London was in the churchyard of St Jude's
Courtfield Gardens. So I took the Underground to Gloucester
Road and found it on the south side of the church, a tall tree, which
had evidently suffered badly in the blitz, many branches being dead;
and though there was a fair amount of leaf there was little or no
sign of flower.

But to return to Kew – on the other side of the Temperate
House I came upon a little holly about nine feet high with large
leaves of dark burnished green, hardly any prickles, and an abundance of green berries, which in due course will turn to that most
cheerful of reds. It well deserves its reputation as one of the very
finest of the green hollies (var. 'Camelliaefolia'). Near it I saw one
of my favourite little trees for the seaside, the tamarisk. It is wonderfully tough and extremely obliging. If you want a hedge all you
have to do is to cut pieces, the length and thickness of a walking-
stick, sharpen them at one end and thrust then in the ground. There
are several pretty tamarisks at Kew, the Mediterranean one being
more thickly covered with tiny blossoms of rosy pink than its kins-
man, the native of England.

Two plants west of the Temperate House were in most charming form that morning, both of the mallow family. One was an elegant little tree of ten feet, *Hoheria lyallii*, from New Zealand, with
leaves of a soft green, greyish underneath, and a wealth of beautiful wide-open white flowers, the petals green at the base and the

stamens in bristling heads. The other was a globe-mallow (*Sphaeralcea*), a small plant smothered delightfully in flower of an unusual light red. Not far away in a large pot was an old trunk with a few flowering shoots. It was the coral-tree from Brazil [*Erythrina crista-galli*], put into a gallery in the Temperate House in the winter and brought out in the summer. The coral-tree stands pruning better than any other leguminous shrub, and every season is cut right back. Its scarlet pea-like flowers are all upside down. Its leaves have a curious hook at their back, and they follow the sun round on a bright day. One of the young gardeners very kindly told me about the plant, and I asked him about himself. He had been trained in a nursery in Scotland, and during the recent war he had gone to sea as cook with the North Sea fishing fleet. I asked how he liked it. Very much he said; so much indeed that he thought of staying on at the job, but after some hesitation he decided to go back to gardening; and now he was very glad that he had made the decision and asked for nothing better than to work on at Kew. His contentment was infectious, and the rest of my walk in the garden I enjoyed more than ever.

Round a corner of the House I was met by a couple of gay old friends: the great Californian Poppy (*Romneya coulteri* var. *trichocalyx*) with its surprisingly large flowers, the petals satiny-white and delicately textured, surrounding a golden crown of massed stamens. Its breath is sweet but not altogether pleasant. No such qualification need be made with regard to the scent of the other plant, *Argyrocytisus battandieri* from the Atlas mountains, with silvery leaves and cylindrical masses of bright yellow flowers, which first appeared in the open in England in Hyde Park in June 1930. It is classed as a broom, but it is not much like the other brooms. Two of these were in full flower in the garden: the Mount Etna broom, with slender green lines of stalk ending in shining yellow vetch-like flowers; and the familiar Spanish broom, its green stems darker and thicker, with scantier flowers. Both of these were effectively massed in beds.

Another bed nearby was very pleasing in the total effect of its innumerable tiny yellow stars of flower: Christ's Thorn, from the Eastern Mediterranean [*Paliurus spina-christi*]. The branches are pliable and very prickly, so that the legend which connects it with the Crown of Thorns is not surprising. But, for a formidable armature of spines, go on a little further and examine the big honey locust from North America [*Gleditsia*]. It was first cultivated in

England about 1700 in the garden of Henry Compton, Bishop of London. It is an interesting tree with its fern-like foliage which turns golden yellow in autumn. Its seed are embedded in sweet pulp (hence its name) in large flat, often twisted, pods, twelve to fifteen inches long. Kew is said to have the finest specimen of honey locust in the country.

In this same part of the garden there are two lovely small chestnuts: the dwarf buckeye from the United States, a great rounded bush covered with erect candles of, as yet, unopened white flowers; and the Californian buckeye, with dense upright panicles of white fragrant flowers, faintly tinged with rose, and just going over. I was walking south towards the Pagoda, and I soon came upon the collection of climbing roses. A small boy passed me, and I heard him say to his mother, "They're dying." But they made a brave show still of pink and white and red. A little further on I stopped to view the solemn avenue of yews, very upright and now ten to twelve feet high: not nearly so impressive as the long avenue of much older yews at Tregrehan in Cornwall. In my own garden at Truro I have four yews grouped round a sundial, in what I must confess is a very drunken attitude. For some reason or other, partly, I think, in order to lean towards the light, they have taken a dissipated slant. At this southern end of Kew before I turned back to the Temperate House I saw a promising *Eucryphia* from Chile. It was *glutinosa*, the hardiest of that small and distinguished family, with little shining dark green leaves and now full of bud. Soon it will be covered all over with large white petals and tufts of conspicuous stamens.

There is no finer cultivator in the world than Mr. C.P. Raffill, who has been in charge of the Temperate House for many years. The House is packed full of interest. Yet I cannot altogether suppress a certain feeling of superiority, as I note plant after plant which I have seen bigger and better in the open air in Cornwall or in the Isles of Scilly. Kew is by no means greatly favoured as regards climate, and the gigantic gas-works just across the river do not add to the purity of the atmosphere. Of the cosseted inmates of the Temperate House, then, I refrain from speaking; and issuing forth again I proceed northwards in a devious course towards the main gate of the garden.

A big sea buckthorn of twenty feet reminds me of a little group which I have planted near the front of my house. It will be long before they attain that size. They have not berried yet to any purpose, and it is a rain of yellow berries that I desire. I like the look of the hop hornbeam, the ironwood[1], with its handsome pyramidal form and its dangling hop-like clusters [*Ostrya carpinifolia*]; and my curiosity is aroused by the *Tetradium*, a neat little tree, discovered by A. Henry in Western China in the year that I was born, now covered with unopened panicles of small greenish yellow buds. And now I am nearing the principal entrance. As I pass a large bed of the *Buddleja* about which Reginald Farrer became so lyrical (*B. alternifolia*). It has not yet done anything with me, but it has evidently flowered well here, and a few little lavender-coloured heads of small flowers are still left open upon it. I marvel at the severity of the pruning of that beautiful *Philadelphus* ('Virginal'). No doubt it is right, and the isolated shoots of new wood which alone are left will produce a vision of dazzling whiteness next year. And now the *Ceanothus* bids me farewell; 'Gloire de Versailles', the favourite, with large spikes of flower but not perhaps so rich a blue as that of others near it – *C.* 'Burkwoodii' and *C.* 'Autumnal Blue'. Through the gate out of this Paradise I go, and on Kew Green I meet the World again.

(*The Guardian*, 10 September 1948, p. 443.)

---

1   Compare page 79. It is the *Ostrya* and *Parrotia* that are more usually known as 'ironwood'.

In the Garden before Christmas

We have had the finest November since I came back to Truro as bishop, thirteen and a half years ago; and if December had come in with a burst of wind and rain we cannot in reason complain. The weather has been so mild and open that the garden has been very slow in going to rest; and plants need rest just as animals and humans do. I am still picking rose-buds. My poor rose bushes will work themselves to death – and my good gardener wheeled nine tons of sweet earth, well supplied with humus, when he renewed their bed and planted afresh four years ago! In Cornwall we are in the habit of cutting off the dead heads of flower on the *Hydrangeas* and relieving the plants of worn-out wood before Christmas, but this year they are so full of sap I hardly dare begin.

My brave old *Brugmansia* has won its race with the weather easily this year. The winter's frost regularly cuts it right to the ground. Nothing daunted, up it comes again, its sappy stalks shooting out at a great rate in early summer, and clothing themselves with large green leaves tasty to caterpillars. If I make war on the caterpillars, or even if I do not, the plant prepares with leisurely dignity its great green and yellow, red-lipped, trumpets of flower; and it is just a question which will appear first, the flowers or the frost.

There are many blossoms now to be seen in the garden, both flowers in season and the late-revellers. Of the latter, the most notable are the *Fuchsias* and my cushion of *Convolvulus sebatius*. As to *Fuchsias* – their name is legion, and it would take an active member of the Fuchsia Society to identify them correctly. I have out a smart flesh-pink and purple which I think is called 'Beauty of Exeter'; and two with Lilliputian flower torches of purple and purple-blue. The convolvulus, which I fetched from the Isles of Scilly, has made itself thoroughly at home and is sprawling over the ground in the freest manner. It keeps its flowers folded till the sun shines and then opens them – pale lavender-blue without, to show an expanse of exquisite blue purple, surrounding a small bunch of white stamens, within. To my astonishment the flowers last well in water, and in a glass gladden my study table ten days together. In season, and doing famously, are the trusty winter jasmine lighting up the walls of the little house where I grow tomatoes with innumerable flowers of a clear and cheerful yellow; and a single chrysanthemum of a brighter yellow still, so generous in blossom that I have asked my gardener to take cuttings that we may have more plants in years to come.

This winter for the first time we have a good flowering of violets – 'Princess of Wales', richly scented both in leaf and flower. The smaller leaves of winter heliotrope (*Petasites*) go well with the blue-purple flowers of the violets, and are often used to save stripping the violet plants. The winter heliotrope counts in the garden as a persistent and ineradicable weed, but its spikes of fragrant lavender purple pay quite sufficient rent for a bank outside.

The garden prize at the moment goes to a young autumn flowering *Prunus*, its graceful branches all snowed with blush pink. Nearby rhododendron 'Christmas Cheer', also blush pink, is trying hard to rival it; while on the other side of the path *Rhododendron* 'Nobleanum', whose pink is brighter but not better, is just beginning its display. So also is the great Winter Sweet on the red wall of the Rose garden. By the end of November it had hardly finished shedding its leaves, but the tiny buttons of horn-yellow with purple centre were already appearing, and no winter scent is more delicious than theirs.

At this time of year I should have berries, but actually I have only a few. My best holly, however, is well furnished. It has two trunks: one bears the usual dark green leaf, the other a leaf with one of the most beautiful variegations I have ever seen. Both trunks this year show a good crop of bright red berries. The best display of berries in the county is found in Mr. George Johnstone's beautiful garden at Trewithen, near Grampound. Here in one bed are three well-established plants of *Viburnum betulifolium*, bent down all through the winter with a vast weight, a veritable cascade, of shining translucent clusters of red berries. The birds luckily do not touch them, so they bring you through to the spring, and any day the sunshine falls upon them they are marvellous to behold.

I have been too busy of late to go into the garden much, but from time to time I sally forth to supply the wood fire in the study, to encourage the collecting of leaves for the compost heap, and to see about a little planting. A fine *Hebe* has just arrived. I saw it in a Naval camp near Torpoint, and the Captain very kindly offered me some of it. It had charming flowers of rather a light blue, and I accepted gratefully. A plant duly arrived, the size of which astonished my gardener, who found the very place at once. And now I am wondering what will be out for Christmas in the Cathedral. Chrysanthemums, I suppose; for the yellow fluff and feathery green of *Acacia baileyana* will not be ready till Epiphany.

(*The Guardian*, 17 December 1948, p. 614.)

The Dangerous Month

The month of February opened with a glorious sunny morning, and after dealing with my correspondence and other immediate business I was delighted to be able to walk slowly round the garden on a leisurely tour of inspection. This is for us one of the tidiest times of the year: the old weeds have mostly died away, and the new ones have not yet appeared. The great exception is that sweet persistent intruder, the Winter Heliotrope. It comes on in advancing waves in spite of our vigorous rearguard actions; and one plant has lifted its smiling defiant face in the very citadel of the rose garden, where, on our best soil, it has thrown up a spike of fragrant purple-and-grey to a height of eighteen inches. It must at all costs be dislodged. Even so, with the paths cleaned up, the bare brown earth and the leafless tracery of twigs and branches on beech and chestnut, the whole scene is neat and restful.

Each year we deal firmly with some part of the garden, rooting up shrubs which are in decline or out of place. This winter we have cleared a little thicket near the house, and planted round it a border of Donard escallonias. With their shining leaves and gay pink flowers they should be just the thing for that windy corner. From the house itself, by command of the diocesan suveyor, we have cleared the Virginia creeper. It was certainly getting too firm a hold, but I doubt if I should have been so readily amenable to diocesan authority if I had not two lovely wisterias already more than making good the loss. On another side of the building we have had to cut right back a climbing hydrangea because it was starving the *Lapageria rosea* given me by the late Canon Boscawen. We cannot afford to risk its amazing funnels of solid pink in November. The time had come also to say good-bye to a very aged friend, a leptospermum, whose tiny white stars of flowers had already grown less of recent years, and its old branches were dying back fast. Here is a choice corner for which I have waiting a tender climbing jasmine.

With a pair of secateurs and a canvas bucket for twigs to light my fire, I set out not long before noon. My first find was some long pieces of bamboo from one of the clumps in the garden. The dead canes broken into small lengths are excellent fire lighters. Near the clump was a large round bush of azalea, sprinkled already with little rosettes of bright purple. I took one as a button-hole, and went on, past my *Magnolia* x *soulangeana*, easiest of all magnolias and now straddling out in rude health over the path, to cut off the dead flowerheads of the only hydrangea left with them. I had attended to the others weeks ago and missed this plant, near a tall holly still richly adorned with its cheerful red berries.

Next, I made my way to the little nursery where I am bringing on plants for my friends and for myself. It lies at the top of a slope, one side of which is damp through the intermittent trickle of a tiny stream. Along this we have planted a line of willows. Two with bright yellow twigs are growing faster than the others, and they are being pruned to make shapely little trees.

In the nursery a *Hoheria* has been left so long that it has turned it into a living room and declines to be dislodged. Very well: it is not such a bad place for it to be after all, and we shall expect to see in due course its pillar of finely-cut greenery bright with a cloud of small white flowers.

A few days earlier we had removed from the nursery a well-grown *Magnolia wilsonii* to its destined home in the sheltered nook in the Cathedral Close. In years to come the delicate white cups of flower hanging from its spreading branches should give a thrill to passers-by in spring.

Truro Cathedral is built low down among the houses in the middle of the town, just south of a shallow stream, and on both sides of the tall building the draught is liable to be chilling and deadly. This, and the loss of our railings in the last war, with the marked preference which the small boys show for our plot of grass above the playing places provided for them by the town authorities, make the problem of beautifying the Close with shrubs and trees nearly insoluble. We had a good young *Prunus hillieri* presented to us a year ago and we planted it with care. But draught and young democracy together have almost done for it. We have now given it first aid, and a companion in *Prunus subhirtella* 'Autumnalis'; and we still cherish a faint hope of seeing the bright pink of the one in spring and the blush pink of the other in late autumn and winter, standing out against the thin grove of ancient ilex which has toughly contended with adversity as long as anyone can remember. Along the west side of the Close we tried some *Escallonia* 'Iveyi', that fine natural hybrid with white flowers which was first recognised by Mr. Ivey, the head gardener in the great garden at Caerhays. But conditions have proved too hard for them; and our next planting must be of *Euonymus japonicus*. That Japanese euonymus makes tall thick hedges in the Isles of Scilly, where its shining leaves are sometimes used as fodder for the cattle. One plant has already been for some years in this bed and looks quite healthy.

To return to Lis Escop garden – the outstanding flowers at the moment are those of daphnes, the heaths and the camellias. The daphnes are *D. odora*, with pink-and-white, deliciously scented rosettes of flower: the larger plant given me by Canon Boscawen, and the smaller is a layer from it. Among the heaths are two large cushions of light purple *Erica* x *darleyensis*, and a white tree heath now grown tall and old and lanky. The camellias in flower are all single pinks of various delicate shades: the double camellias will be out later. Below the vegetable garden there is a path with a wide border of shrubs on either side. Here on the east are the wytch-hazel with spidery yellow blossoms along the bare branches, two grevilleas, both the yellow-flowered and the lovely pink; and, near the largest sweet chestnut in the county, a little bush of *Sarcococca hookeriana* var. *humilis*. *Sarcoccoca* has fresh green foliage, will stand shade, and though its flowers are minute, they have a most power-ful fragrance. There are two large plants of it in Ludgvan rectory garden that astonish you with rich waves of scent as you pass by. On the west side, the hypericum from Rowallane is still – marvel-lous to relate – definitely in flower. It has been giving a rich display of its great yellow saucers for months. Further along, *Oemleria cerasi-formis*, the Oso Berry from the United States, is just beginning to show its small, white, almond-scented blossoms.

In other parts of the garden the two earliest pink rhododen-drons are still good, and others – large rhododendrons of the arboreum species – are coming on to take their place. R. 'The Countess of Haddington' is covered with lovely tapering buds of a delicate yellowish green. As I approached my little *Cornus florida* f. *rubra*, which is yet too young to flower, a friendly robin cocked his eye at me from its leafless twigs; and close by the sun shone brightly on the rich clusters of berries on a pair of skimmias.

Of all the indications of the winter's mildness the most sur-prising are the thick waxen-lipped red and yellow trumpets still dan-gling from the sprawling brugmansia against the wall of the rose garden. And when my gardener joined me his sharp eye observed the swelling fruit buds on the blackcurrants and the plum-trees. Dangerously advanced, he thought them, and told me of an aged friend who had said that he never remembered such a January since the one in the year when it was followed by the great blizzard in March. "We shall pay for this", my gardener added ferociously. If so, I thought, then let us enjoy it now: and we did thoroughly enjoy it that still shining morning. For me payment began at once: with two long Governing Body meetings in the afternoon, followed by a night journey to London.

(*The Guardian*, 25 February 1949, p. 94.)

The Bridal Dress of Spring

Spring, the young bride of the year, chooses always a white wedding. Distinguished guests like camellias, magnolias or rhododendrons, are allowed pink or red, and late-comers, like the bluebells, some other colour; but the bride herself is in shining white with a bouquet of soft yellow.

This year the season has been early and, thanks to mild and dry weather, flowers of every sort have been abundant. Within a week of Lady Day, sheets of white blackthorn have been lighting up the hedgerows: very common and familiar, but how very beautiful! Chiming in with them along the lanes are the frequent clumps of stitchwort, each frail white flower nodding its head at every breath of wind.

In my garden the earliest magnolia to flower is *M. stellata*. My plant is the tallest *M. stellata* I know. It is on the side of a rising path and towers above it, a great shield of snow white, glistening in the sunshine. Its flowers have twelve to eighteen long strap-shaped petals, with a very pleasant aromatic fragrance, especially, I think, at night. Other magnolias also seem to be more fragrant by night than by day. *M. sargentiana* var. *robusta* is an example. I saw an immense spreading tree of it in a garden near Penzance in the last week but one of March. It had hundreds of enormous flowers of pale pink on its bare branches. "An over-loaded Christmas tree", said a lady irreverently. But what a Christmas tree, and what a load!

The Sunday after, in the rectory garden of St Just-in-Roseland, on the east side of Falmouth harbour, I saw the pure white flowers of *Magnolia denudata*. It is the lily tree which the Chinese have cultivated for 1,300 years. That well-kept garden, let me add, is a fine example of what can be accomplished by a keen rector and an equally keen wife with no outside help.

So much must suffice for the whites, and now for the yellows. The Horticultural Colour Chart includes some eighteen yellows. "Primrose yellow" has been a colour name for over 300 years. There is no more delightful sight in spring than the high hedges of a Cornish lane studded with rosettes of yellow primroses; and they go on flowering and flowering for weeks and weeks. Primrose yellow also are the various species of *Corylopsis* from the Far East. Their pendant spikes of fragrant flowers have a cowslip-like fragrance. *C. pauciflora* is similar and charming. Best of all, I think,

5   *Bishop Hunkin with his* Magnolia stellata.

is *C. sinensis* var. *calvescens*. I have recently seen two or three large bushes of these heavenly plants holding out a rain of delicate blossom, radiant primrose in the sunlight.

Much stronger yellows are the daffodils, new varieties of which are constantly being produced by Cornish and other growers. 'King Alfred', that great yellow trumpet raised by John Kendall, did not flower till after his death (1890). My favourite of all is 'Trevithian', raised at Lanarth by the late P.D. Williams, a charming clean-yellow jonquil with a delicious scent. There are, of course, other colours: that fine white trumpet 'Beersheba', for example, raised by one of the pioneers of the art, the Rev. George Herbert Engleheart (1857–1936). There are even pink daffodils – I cannot abide them.

In my garden I have two sizeable forsythias of the best sort; but I never see the dazzle of yellow on them which I see in many other gardens, for most of the buds are eaten by audacious blue tits which strip the branches almost bare. I fare better with the bright yellow buttons of the double *Kerria japonica*; and I like the single kerria better still. Its small open saucers of butter-yellow have a more distinguished air.

Rhododendron macabeanum, with its huge leaves surrounding grand trusses of flower, is, in its best form a delicate yellow. There was a noble specimen in the Cornwall Spring Flower Show in the first week of April. Winter's Bark, *Drimys winteri*, the bitter aromatic bark of which was brought home in 1578 by Winter, one of Drake's captains, from the Magellan Straits (he had found it an antidote to scurvy), has flowered superlatively this year. I saw a tree 40 feet tall on the west shore of Falmouth Harbour, with hundreds of clusters of cream flowers amongst its small, bright, pale green leaves. There are even taller trees elsewhere in West Cornwall – up to 60 feet in height.

Many other notabilities grace the nuptials of the spring, but two more only will I mention; both, not in the garden but in the wild: the gorse, always reliable, bursts of it, blazes of it, here, there and everywhere, of great cheer to the dejected spirit; and the pussy willow. Never have I seen it in such gay form, of a nondescript greenish-yellow, but with a most engaging pussiness.

(*The Guardian*, 23 April 1949, p. 184.)

Spring Flowers in Galilee

In "Diplomat in Peace and War" Sir Hughe Knatchbull-Hugessen has given a most interesting account of his experiences in a number of very different countries. He himself is the son of a Sussex parson; and one of the most striking passages in his book is concerned with Palestine:

> In Jerusalem there is only one thing visible which satisfies the wish to establish contact with the most ancient times, something which cannot have changed. It is to be found in the Dome of the Rock, in the precincts of what was Solomon's Temple, the scene of so much of the life and teaching of Christ. The beauty and symmetry of that extraordinary building cannot be ignored and the huge natural rock which it shelters gives the sure conviction of something immeasurably ancient and enduring which has played a part in the birth of faith in a Single Deity, and which has witnessed the times when human faith was in its infancy.

"The Christian will do better", Sir Hughe continues, "to go to Galilee"; and his description of Galilee is illustrated by a charming black-and-white sketch of *Tiberias and the Lake*:

> The general appearance of the country around the lake
> has certainly changed, but its chief features remain. There
> is nothing left of Capernaum but the ruins of the syna-
> gogue; the "coasts of Decapolis" are there but not the ten
> cities. Nevertheless, the lake, the river and the hills are the
> same. So must the flowers be. Galilee and the lake are
> especially favoured in the spring. The deep depression
> below sea level gives an almost tropical climate in which
> nature revels. The countryside is literally covered with wild
> flowers. Nowhere else in the world have I seen such a
> wealth of colour. The spring flowers in Persia are more
> scattered, the tulips and irises have a hard soil and a hot
> sun to cope with. But here the flowers seem to take con-
> trol and dominate the entire scene.
>   In these surroundings it is easier to think back. Like
> the Rock in Jerusalem the scenery of Galilee gives a sense
> of reality. The débris of later centuries does nor interfere,
> the New Testament story stands out in clear simplicity.
> One is tempted to study that life in the light of this reality,
> by the cold dispassionate historical method, putting aside
> all suspicion of emotion. It loses nothing, rather it seems
> to affirm itself more strongly by this approach than by
> doctrines such as the Immaculate Conception, the Virgin
> Birth or even the Resurrection in its purely material form.
> These tend to place Him out of our reach, to separate the
> Divine and the human into watertight compartments with
> no passing from one to the other. To human beings this
> can only bring frustration and discouragement. It seems a
> pity that the curtain of mystery and mysticism is not
> drawn aside to show Him more often as the *reductio* – or
> better still, the *productio ad perfectum* of the good which is
> implanted also in our own natures. As to His own nature,
> it seems to be only a question of approach. Perfection,
> whether it be reached by a painful upward ascent or mani-
> fested from above, is still perfection. It is a blend of the
> Divine and the human: no one can say where are the
> beginning and the end.

Here indeed is food for thought both theological and botanical. The plants that flower to-day in Galilee must many of them be the direct descendants of those that were flowering there in the first century of our era. Every year from babyhood to young man there burst upon Jesus the miracle of the spring. In Galilee it is a burst indeed. All the flowers, or nearly all, seem to come together about April, and before the end of June they are gone: sweet, sudden revelation of divine beauty, short-lived like the Lord Himself. "Consider the lilies of the field, how they grow", He said; "they toil not neither do they spin: and yet I say unto you, that even Solomon in all his glory was not arrayed like one of these" (Mt. vi, 28, 29: Lk xii, 27, 28). The Greek word is the ordinary word for "lily" and the term "wild lily" might include a number of plants. Something individually stately and regal seems to be indicated: asphodels on the hillside glistening against the lake; or purple gladiolus overtopping the corn, or the purple and white iris of Nazareth. One of these would fit the passage in the Gospels better than the scarlet anemone favoured by Canon Tristram; for the saying continues "Wherefore, if God so clothe the grass in the field, which today is and tomorrow is cast into the oven..." The suggestion of fuel brings to mind the upright stalks of asphodel, iris, or gladiolus more readily than the low growing anemone.

Of all the lovely flowers honoured by the fellah with the name *hannun* (i.e. *beautiful wild flower*) the scarlet anemone would be his first choice. The plain of Gennesaret is "red with remembrance of the Anemones", their period of flowering being from Christmas to April, and there are white and mauve anemones as well as red. The crocus, yellow and white, begins early too. It is seen on the hill behind Nazareth in December. The yellow and white Narcissus (*N. tazetta*) with its arrowy fragrancy also starts in December and goes on to February. It is generally identified with the Rose of Sharon (Canticles, ii 1). Deeper yellow to orange is provided by the crowfoot, and a little later the handsome corn-marigold is yellow-bright. Very gay are the tulips, especially the scarlet one with a blackish spot at the base of its sepals. Red also are the poppies on the plains in April, while blues are provided by the dark-blue cornflower, the small blue iris, the grape hyacinth and masses of borage. More delicate in texture and colouring are the pink flax, the cyclamen from white to deep pink among the rocks, and *Ricotia lunaria*, a pretty little pink crucifer, peculiar to Palestine. *Onosma echioides* (Golden Drop) swings its yellow bells on the Galilean hills, the shrubby *Lavatera* (*L. trimestris*) is lavish with its large pink, mallow-like flowers, and water lilies, white and yellow, grow in still water, especially on the little lake to the north of the Sea of Galilee, lake Huleh. Hosts of other flowers there are, but these must suffice for our miniature picture; and we must not forget the shrubs and flow-ering trees. Half a dozen may serve as examples. Let the first be the beautiful white broom (*Retama raetam*), the bush under which the prophet Elijah sank exhausted, quite wrongly in 1 Kings xix, 4, called the *juniper*. The second and third shall be the Oleander [*Nerium o.*] with dark green leaves and bright pink fragrant blossoms by the Sea of Galilee, and the thorny burnet (*Poterium spinosum*) with small serrated leaves, deep red blossoms and sharp thorns, promi-nent in the thickets. For the others let there be mentioned the *Styrax* (*S.officinale*) with it fragrant white flowers with yellow stamens and dark green leaves silver on the under side, which may be seen side by side with the hawthorn in full flower together in the woods in the middle of March; the various kinds of wild almond, and finally the common myrtle, evergreen and aromatic, with small white flowers.

The burst of blossoming in Galilee coincides with the burst of triumph in the Christian year; and in the joyful chorus of Creation the flowers have a glorious part.

(*The Guardian*, 24 June 1949, p. 292.)

The Seaside Book

It is just a hundred years since William Henry Harvey published the first edition of *The Seaside Book*, in which he gave a short popular account of the natural history of the seashore: birds, maritime veg-etation, marine animals, seaweeds, and so on. "The numerous marine watering-places", he wrote,

> which are thronged in the summer and autumn months, ought to be so many schools for naturalists ... There is no need to import the winter resources of cities – balls, parties, and theatrical representations – to the watering-place. Half the year ought to suffice for these amuse-ments. Let the summer and seaside preserve their native

pleasures undisturbed. There is so much to be enjoyed
on the seashore when the mind is once opened to the
pleasures afforded by the study of natural history, that
no other stimulus is wanted to keep the interest of the
visitor constantly awake.

Dr. Harvey continued,

our conception of the Author of Nature may be diffuse –
a vague idea of some illimitable Power, in ceaseless action;
but the more we pursue this delightful study, the more we
recognize, if we work in a proper spirit, proofs of the
personality of God. Though now we can know Him but
in part, and only see Him reflected in His works, as it
were, 'through a glass, darkly', we look forward to a time
when we shall behold Him 'face to face', and shall know
Him 'even as we ourselves are known'.

The Seaside Book was very well received, and went through four
editions (the fourth in 1857). It is pleasantly written, and contains
a number of vignettes, the one at the head of the first chapter
showing the ruined oratory of St Perran in the sandhills near
Perranporth in Cornwall.

In the year following the publication of *The Seaside Book*,
Harvey began a correspondence with another naturalist, Mrs.
Margaret Gatty. They corresponded for ten years before they
finally met. Mrs. Gatty was the younger of the two daughters of the
Rev. Alexander Scott, Chaplain to Horatio Nelson. Dr Scott was
devoted to Nelson. "What will you think of me", he wrote to his
uncle, Admiral Scott, after Trafalgar, "who detest this victory? It
has deprived me of my beloved and adored friend." Dr. Scott
retired from the Navy to a Yorkshire vicarage, and named his first
child Horatia. His wife died when Horatia was only three and
Margaret only two, and he remained a widower till his death at the
age of seventy-two. He filled his house as he had previously filled
his cabin, with books. Every volume was bought because he wanted to read it, for he was a voracious and very miscellaneous reader.
He never sent his daughters to school, but they pursued their own
studies among "the books" and taught their dolls according to their
hobbies – one the geography of Spain, another the Greek declen-
sions. A hundred and ten years ago this month (July 8, 1839)

Margaret married the Rev. Alfred Gatty, D.D., Vicar of Ecclesfield, also in Yorkshire, and there the remainder of her life was spent. She handed on the tradition of writing for children to her own daughter, Juliana Horatia, afterwards Mrs. Ewing, whose children's books became yet more famous than her mother's.

Mrs. Gatty and her friend, Dr. Harvey, were alike not only in their religious appreciation of nature and in their pleasant sense of humour, but also in the extraordinary cheerfulness and courage with which they faced illness and suffering and death itself. Harvey was brought up a Quaker, and it was only after prolonged thought and prayer that he decided at the age of thirty-five to be baptised (on Ash Wednesday, February 25, 1846, in St. Mark's church, Dublin). He became a strong and loyal Churchman. He was much interested in the Universities Mission to Central Africa. "A great and glorious undertaking", he wrote after hearing Bishop Mackenzie in Dublin. He loved the English Liturgy and distinguished "good" from "bad" "Pussey-cats", as he called the followers of Pusey. He would not have the former maligned, and was well aware that some people preferring "a laxer rule than the Church has ordained" were ready to "cry 'Puseyism, Puseyism' at what is really only sober Church of England after all".

Harvey is the greatest of all Irish botanists. He travelled extensively in South Africa, the United States, Australia and New Zealand; and he was an indefatigable writer. Among his greatest works are *Flora Capensis*, an account of the plants of Cape Colony and Natal, and a *History of British Seaweeds* in four volumes with 360 coloured plates, all drawn on the stone by his own hand. Harvey wrote also on the Algae of North America and Australia. Indeed, he was in his own day the greatest living authority on Algae. Next time I go to Tresco and see there the very striking South African bush *Greyia sutherlandii*, with its bright scarlet flowers and long showy stamens, I shall think of Harvey; for the plant was named by him and Sir William Hooker after Sir George Grey, Governor General of the Cape Colony, and the discoverer of the species, Dr. Peter Sutherland, Surveyor General of Port Natal. Harvey himself visited Tresco (in the autumn of 1858), where he admired the great hedges of geraniums and the multitude of Australian, Cape of Good Hope, New Zealand and Californian plants. "Some shrubs", he wrote, "rarely seen in England here form thickets." Mrs. Gatty also visited the Isles of Scilly on one occasion with her husband, and never forgot the bright colours of the mesembryanthemums.

The first series of her *Parables from Nature*, probably the work for which she is most remembered, was published in 1855. Mrs. Gatty had by this time been corresponding with Dr Harvey for about five years, and consulted him on various points – for example, about the "Red snow plant". The first series of parables was followed by others – five series in all. Besides these and a number of children's books, Mrs. Gatty also wrote, under Dr. Harvey's supervision, a book on British Seaweeds (1862).

Both the friends were in many respects very modern and progressive. Thus Harvey wrote to Mrs. Gatty (July 18, 1860), "I cannot believe that Scientific facts are revealed in Scripture, and I think that much mischief is done by striving to find them there." Mrs. Gatty was greatly interested in the introduction of chloroform, and took chloroform from her doctor in order to overcome the suspicion against it.

For fifty years Dr. Harvey remained a bachelor, and then in the spring of 1861 he married Miss Phelps of Limerick. They were very happy together, but almost immediately his health began to break down. He was staying at Torquay when on May 15, 1866, he died, and by his own desire he was buried in the cemetery there. "Where the tree falls, there let it lie", he had said. "It never appeared to me to be of any consequence where we die or where we are buried. The work is a mere speck in the universe." On the day before his death he had written to a friend: "I do not think that I shall last very much longer. I pray to be preserved in the waiting spirit, which has hitherto supported me. I am thankful to be spared acute pain, and the Lord has been very gracious in preserving my mind calm and clear. I can trust Him to the end."

By 1866 Mrs. Gatty's health had begun to fail too. She suffered great pain but bore it with the utmost courage and resignation. "Tell him he is not to pray that I may have less pain, but more patience", was the message she sent to a friend who had promised his prayers. She died on October 5, 1873.

(*The Guardian*, 22 July 1949, p. 346.)

The Thirsty Land

We have all been enjoying the bright sunshine for many weeks, though some have sometimes been in two minds about the heat. There is no pleasing everybody. But the gardens have been very dry. And what is the effect of prolonged drought in the garden? Lammas Day (August 1) is a good day on which to go round and see. It was a day of Loaf Mass in medieval England: that is, for the offering of the first fruits of the harvest. And the harvest is well forward this year, though on Lammas Day itself the fields were damp and harvesters were at liberty to break off and look at their gardens. The first thing in the garden that strikes the roving eye is the comparative fewness of the weeds: comparative, I say, not superlative. My garden has not in recent summers reached even the comparative degree before, and it is never likely to attain the superlative. This year, however, we have made special efforts, and the weather has been of great assistance. For instance: the half dozen rows of raspberries are unfortunately in a plot infected by bindweed. The right thing to do is to remove the rows to another part of the garden, to dig the whole piece up and eradicate every vestige of that creeping, crawling, white fleshy root. But that was too drastic this year. So what I did was to sustain constant attacks on the intruder, pulling at it wherever it appeared, in the hope of bleeding it – not to death, that would be too much to hope, but to degeneracy. That plan, thanks largely to the dryness of the soil, has been to a considerable extent effective; and if the raspberries have given us only a moderate crop that has not been due to any throttling by bindweed.

It has been a lovely year so far for flowers. The flowers of the spring smothered shrub and bush, and they were fine and large. The flowers of the summer are equally plentiful, but they tend to be smaller. This is very noticeable, for example, in the case of that neat and dependable hebe with box-like leaves and closely packed clusters of white flowers, and also with the hydrangeas, unless they happen to be in a shady, moist place. Most of my hydrangeas are of an intense, cool, refreshing, blue; and perhaps the most elegant of all, 'Blue Wave', is just coming into full flower.

It has been a grand year for honeysuckles. There have been masses of honeysuckle for weeks and weeks along the hedgerows, and no garden honeysuckle can beat them. The scent of my

Etruscan honeysuckle, however, which flowered this year for the first time, was outstandingly gorgeous. One of my study windows is wreathed profusely with a yellow-and-white honeysuckle from China, gay and fragrant enough, though hardly up to the best English. Alongside it is the star-jasmine [*J. officinale*], also from China, with little clusters of white flowers whose delicate scent is one of the most delicious of all. Another Chinese climber, *Jasminum polyanthum*, is somewhat tender. It came to me from the great garden at Tresco in the Isles of Scilly, and it was only planted out against a very sheltered corner of the house this Spring. The weather has just suited it. It has romped ahead amazingly and is now producing its very fragrant and beautiful white flowers about 7 feet up the wall. Another trailing plant that has thoroughly enjoyed this glowing summer is my African convolvulus [*sebatius*]. It is forming a fast-spreading mat of light green foliage starred with funnel-shaped flowers of a marvellous violet-blue. It is very regular in its daily habits, and, wet or fine, dull or shine, it opens its flowers about eight in the morning and folds them again about five in the afternoon.

Another advantage of this dry summer has been the diminution of snails and slugs, though this is partly due to our dusting the bottom of our walls with D.D.T. – the bottom only, to avoid poisoning the diligent and welcome bee. A day or two ago I had unfortunately to massacre a dozen and a half of these gastropod molluscs which I found lurking in damp cracks below my little lily pond.

So far I have been reckoning the credit side of the drought: now for the debit. The most notable rhododendron in the garden *R. falconeri*, with large trusses of white flowers and huge leaves with a rich brown tomentum on their underside, showed alarming signs of distress and had to be given an emergency ration of water. At the back of the house I planted a few years ago a couple of those strong climbers from North Eastern Asia *Celastrus orbiculatus*. They have not yet shown the beauty of their brilliantly-coloured fruit, but they have grown vigorously to a height of more than 10 feet: and now suddenly one of the pair has withered and died. The main reason is lack of depth of soil so close to the house and the *Celastrus* is a gross feeder; but no doubt the drought has accelerated the sad decease. The long border of 'Princess of Wales' violets which had filled that part of the garden with fragrance most of the winter was severely attacked by the red spider, and we have not been able to deal with it at all effectively.

The chief disadvantage from the prolonged dryness of the soil, however, will not be felt till next winter. We may then be very short of winter vegetables: broccoli, beetroot, carrots and so on; for the drought has put us perhaps a month behind. Five times my persevering gardener has sown carrots, but his first failures were due not so much to the drought as to the rabbits. So impudent were the attacks of these creatures that I had to find him a gun, and within the last few months he has accounted for sixteen (big and little). Not that these are the only predatory animals with which we have had to contend. One night four cattle broke into the garden from a neighbouring field and left their deep hoof-prints all over the place. Mercifully the damage they did, considering the large area of their invasion, was surprisingly small.

Below the tennis court, in the least dry part of the garden, where the soil has been worked up particularly well this year, thirteen rows of peas interspersed with other vegetables have come up without a gap or failure in a most pleasing pattern of green. The County Horticultural Adviser, who is a great authority (and a clergyman's daughter) said that the bed really ought to be photographed. That has not been done, but we are wearing the feathers she gave us in our caps, especially as vegetables generally appear just now to be in short supply. This was evident from the entries in the Garden Show held last week in connexion with one of the Truro parish churches (St. George's). An admirable little show it was, and the standard of the exhibits was remarkably high; with lovely sweet peas and pom-pom peonies, gooseberries as big as plums and runner-beans whose immense length did not impare their edibility. And what a success it was as a social event – everybody so friendly and pleased, and any profit to go to the funds of the church! The same delightful atmosphere was observable at a similar Church Horticultural Show at Camborne a few weeks previously. And there have been several others. May the number increase! Is not the fruitage of a garden better than the shuffling of a whist-drive or the trampling of a dance?

(*The Guardian*, 12 August 1949, p. 376.)

Makers of British Botany

One of the best methods of studying the development of an important subject is the biographical method. A very interesting book published by the Cambridge University Press shortly before the war of 1914–18 under the title *Makers of British Botany* consists of a collection of short biographies. It was edited by Dr. F.W. Oliver, and his table of contents mentioned the names of seventeen distinguished botanists, beginning with Robert Morrison (1620–1683) and ending with Sir Joseph Dalton Hooker (1817–1911). It is worthy of note that of these seventeen, four were clergymen of the Church of England, three were sons of clergymen and one of a Congregational minister, while a ninth, William Henry Harvey (1811–1866), was one of the most devout Churchmen. It has long been recognized that the parsonage has produced great gardeners, but perhaps it has not been so widely realized that the clergy and their closest relatives and friends have played a leading part in the more strictly scientific field of botany.

The succession of clerical botanists covers the three centuries. First comes John Ray (1627–1705). He was the son of an Essex blacksmith, and became a Fellow of Trinity College, Cambridge, in 1649. An illness the following year made it necessary for him to rest and walk in the country. "First the rich array of spring-time meadows, then the shape, colour and structure of particular plants fascinated and absorbed me: botany became a passion." "By his chamber" (in Trinity College), a friend wrote, "he hath a little garden which is as full of choice things as it can hold: that it were twenty time as big I could wish for his sake." Ray was ordained in London in December, 1660, and forfeited his fellowship on St. Bartholomew's Day, 1662, under the Act of Uniformity. As a naturalist he toured Western Europe, and he travelled Britain so thoroughly that he could supply first hand a list of the rarer plants for every English county. He is indeed the first great English naturalist. "He is a person of great worth; and yet humble, and far from conceitedness and self-admiring ... a conscientious Christian; and that's much said in little", wrote one of his friends, John Worthington, Master of Jesus College. For evidence of Ray's outstanding genius reference may be made to the monumental biography published during the recent war (1942) by Dr. Charles Raven, Master of Christ's.

Next on our list chronologically is Stephen Hales (1677–1761), the father of physiology. As a Fellow of Corpus Christi College Cambridge, he began to work at chemistry in what he called "the elaboratory in Trinity College." Subsequently he was for fifty-two years perpetual curate of Teddington, where he not only carried out his scientific researches but was a very faithful parish priest. His friends used to speak of his constant serenity and cheerfulness of mind. "He could look even upon ... those who did him unkind offices, without any emotion of particular indignation; not from want of discernment or sensibility; but he used to consider them only like those experiments which, upon trial, he found could never be applied to any useful purpose, and which he therefore calmly and dispassionately laid aside." He used to teach the housewives of his parish to place an inverted tea-cup at the bottom of their pies and tarts "to prevent the syrop from boiling over and to preserve the juice."

The research for which Stephen Hales is best known is that on the transpiration of plants, and he carried out his first experiment on a sunflower growing in a flower pot. It was to Stephen Hales that John Wesley was referring when he said, "how well do philosophy and religion agree in a man of sound understanding."

The third clergyman in the list of Makers of British Botany is John Stevens Henslow (1796–1861). Henslow was an all-round man. He was only twenty-six when he was appointed Professor of Mineralogy at Cambridge. He resigned this professorship and became Professor of Botany in 1827. He was an inspiring teacher, and always had "demonstrations" from living specimens.

In 1838 he became Rector of Hitcham. Here he encouraged the study of botany in the village school and taught the children how to dry plants. He also tried to interest the farmers of the neighbourhood in applying science to the methods of cultivation. In 1845–46, the year of the potato famine in Ireland, all the potatoes in the rectory garden were rotten with disease, but the rector recovered from them at least two sacks of starch. One of his children took a sponge cake to school made with this potato flour and astonished his master by telling him that it was made out of rotten potatoes.

The fourth of these clerical Makers of British Botany, the Rev. Miles Berkeley (1803–1889), was a pioneer in the field of plant pathology. He, too, was a Cambridge man (of Christ's College). His first curacy was at Margate, where he took up the study of seaweeds. Later he turned his attention to fungi, and for nearly half a century practically all collections of exotic fungi passed through his hands. He was the first to recognize the importance of investigating plant diseases caused by fungi, and he himself worked out the life history of the fungus which is the cause of potato murrain. This study he followed with a series of others, including an investigation of the vine-mildew. Berkeley was a man of great refinement. He had a tall commanding figure, but he was very modest and retiring, and he was only elected a Fellow of the Royal Society at the age of seventy-six.

Limitations of space forbid any account of the other five botanists to whom reference was made at the beginning of this article: and these brief notes on these four distinguished clergy must suffice to illustrate the long and honourable connexion of the English clergy with the science of botany.

(*The Guardian*, 2 September 1949, p. 415.)

On-coming Autumn

The days are still bright and hot, but in the early morning and in the evening there is the characteristic tang of autumn in the air. Among the masses of green, brown leaves are appearing and strewing themselves upon the grass. It is time to look out for nuts and berries; and Harvest Festivals are close at hand.

Early spring is the best time in Cornish gardens, and owing to the general mildness of summers as well as winters we do not expect the blaze of autumn colouring which is just preparing to show itself in the great arboretum at Westonbirt and in various degrees in the Midlands and Eastern counties. At the moment the herbaceous border should afford the forefront of the garden's display, but here in the Bishop's garden the herbaceous border has been turned into a shrub border, and the flowering of most of the shrubs is over.

Nevertheless flowers we still have. Let me describe the most outstanding. None are more striking than the score of pink funnels dangling from the climbing, thin, wiry branches of *Lapageria rosea* upon a shady north wall. The stuff of each funnel is so solidly beautiful, and the surface within is like pink frozen snow. The African *Convolvulus* [*sebatius*] has enjoyed this hot, waterless summer, and its abundant tubes of lovely purplish blue open wide with exquisite freshness day by day. Near it a very small *Senna* [*corymbosa*] has produced a corymb or two of bright yellow flower to show its joyful anticipation of the future. This *Senna* from Argentina is tender in England, and I have lost it twice. The present plant represents the third attempt. There are plenty of hydrangeas still blue with flower, but they are a good deal past their prime and look a little nonplussed from lack of water. Perhaps our chief stand-by just now is the family of fuchsias. They cheerfully dangle their showy flowers in various sizes and shades of purple and red and white. The mild winter gave them an unusually good start, and they have never looked back. At this time of the year they are the characteristic shrub of cottage gardens in the west. Keeping pace with them is the more uncommon Californian fuchsia called after an eighteenth-century professor (Zauschner) [now *Epilobium*] with small, linear, ash-grey leaves on long, woody, arching stems, and sprays of scarlet tubular flowers. Of a rather similar habit but several sizes larger is the Bush Clover from Japan (*Lespedeza*). From its swaying wands hang rose-purple flowers in long drooping racemes. It looks particularly charming when over-shadowing the numerous fringed, electric-blue flowers of *Caryopteris* x *clandonensis*, as I saw it in another garden a few days ago. These two plants I find two of the most reliable of the small minority of shrubs whose time of flowering is in the autumn. Another which has the great additional attraction of a rich aromatic scent is a Mexican *Ageratina* (*ligustrina*). Its clusters of whitish flowers are much beloved by Red Admiral butterflies, as also are the long, slender, purple panicles of the *Buddlejas*. In America the *Buddleja* is known as the Butterfly Bush. *Buddlejas* of various sorts have been flowering profusely here in England for weeks. No shrub from abroad makes itself more quickly or thoroughly at home. Its seeds are borne far and wide by the wind, and it has appeared in force on many of the bombed sites in London. *Buddleja globosa* has, as its name implies, globes of honey-scented orange-yellow flowers, and I have a couple of specimens of the interesting cross between this and the more common *Buddleja* with the long flower sprays. My search for autumn-flowering shrubs a few years ago took me to the *Perovskia* [*atriplicifolia*] from Afghanistan with scented, grey leaves of upright spikes of violet-blue flowers from August to October. But it asks for more heat than Cornwall can supply, and even this hot summer its performance has been skimpy. The trailing knotweed from the Himalayas (*Polyganum vacciniifolium*) has likewise disappointed me. I greatly admired its minute forest of spikes of bright rose-coloured flowers some years ago at Wisley, but it by no means shows its paces here. Evidently I have not put it in the right place. To the Trumpet-Vine (*Campsis radicans*) from the south-eastern United States I have certainly given one of the best places I could. The gorgeous beauty of its scarlet and orange trumpet flowers must have attracted the attention of some of the first settlers, for it was cultivated in England in 1640. My plant is an old one and responds only to hot summers. This year it has been so disobliging as to produce its flowers at the very top, most of them dangling the wrong side of the wall. Happily I caught sight of them as I went out in my car by the back drive, or I might have missed them altogether. The flat, purplish, beautifully constructed Passion Flowers against another sheltered wall also nearly escaped me. They were so few and high up, the plant never having fully recovered from the severe frosts of two or three winters ago.

Now is the time for Belladonna lilies [*Amaryllis*], each solid fleshy, dark pink stem supporting an umbel of fresh pink flower. I have a dozen just beginning, but mine are late. A charming clump springing from the very path close to the south-east wall of St. Paul's church on the road into Truro from the north, is just over. In such a situation Belladonnas are quite perfect.

In addition to these flowers whose proper time is now, there are many remnants and survivors. Dark red and red-yellow *Abutilons*, the small pink-and-white tubes of *Abelia*, the yellow saucers of a shrubby St. John's Wort, strong wisps of honeysuckle and a few sprigs of the very fragrant white star-jasmine are notable examples. A small *Kalmia* [*angustifolia*] is displaying for a second time this year its tiny porcelain cups of flower of exquisite texture but a not very attractive purple-pink. *Magnolia* x *soulangeana* is still sprinkled with its large flowers of purple and white; and the ancient *Magnolia grandiflora* against the south wall of the house is holding aloft several great chalices of fragrant cream.

So much for the flowering trees and shrubs. Though, as I have said, we have no proper herbaceous border we have a few herbaceous plants scattered about. They give welcome little splashes of colour, but none of them need be particularly mentioned here. I would rather end with a word or two about berries and fruits. Of these the two most striking at the moment are the dark blue globular oblongs on the *Billardiera* [*longiflora*], a Tasmanian climber just outside my study window, and the bright red bottle-shaped hips of *Rosa Moyesii*. The berries of the South American *Pernettya* [*mucrona-*

ta] are just beginning to colour, and the fruit cylinders of *Magnolia wilsonii* are unpeeling and displaying the scarlet-coated seeds within. The Bladder-Senna [*Colutea arborescens*] has long been decorated with its brown, bladder seed pods as well as its yellow and brown pea-like flowers: now the seed pods alone are left. There is a plentiful harvest of cobnuts, for my skilful gardener has pruned the trees [*Corylus avellana*] into the good nut-bearing bowl-like shape. From an upper window the orange berries of a *Pyracantha* just below against the house are a bright surprise. The *Pittosporums* have black seed in plenty in sweet little green boxes: the mouse-like seed-capsules of the winter-sweet are hidden among its yet unfallen leaves: and a handful of bright red berries on a young group of the best-berrying *Viburnum* [*betulifolium*] raises the hope of shining cascades of beauty in autumns to come.

(*The Guardian*, 30 September 1949, p. 466.)

Winter Treasures in the Garden

Here in Cornwall December is generally mild. So in the rose garden rosebuds will still be opening, pink and red: flowers will be left on the honeysuckle: there may be a few light violet spikes upon a *Hebe*, and even a belated red geranium. I must not linger over such fragments, charming though they be. But before I go on to the solid-treasure of the season I must just mention a beautiful border-line case: the *Eupatorium* which keeps on changing its name. It has changed three times at least within the last few years – let us call it *Ageratina ligustrina*, as most recent catalogues do. Its home is in the Mexican forests, and it is not hardy at Kew, but it has done well here and goes on into December producing its flat round clusters of whitish flower-buds, pleasantly aromatic, and very attractive to Red Admiral butterflies.

The main treasures of the garden so far this winter have been seven in number. First I put the big Wintersweet against the old, red-brick wall. It does not need so sheltered a place, but it shows its gratitude every year with thousands of little horn-coloured flowers with purple centres along its bare branches. I am continually cutting pieces which fill a room with their delicious fragrance. This plant was in the garden long before I came in 1935. The six others I have planted myself – and latest the violets, 'Princess of Wales', in a longer border. The leaves are scented as well as the large dark purple flowers, so that the perfume floats up to surprise the passer-by.

The most distinguished of the seven is undoubtedly *Camellia oleifera* with wide open flowers consisting of white petals circled round a cluster of golden stamens. I planted two in 1945, and I did not expect them to flower so soon and so luxuriantly. They are slender creatures and I hope they are not overdoing it: but their green leaves are bright with health and the flowers have a distinct, though not very strong, pleasant scent. More pronounced and more delicious is the lily-of-the-valley fragrance of the long racemes of tiny yellow flowers on *Mahonia japonica*. It is a formidable looking shrub, standing up on tough stalks with prickles and dark green pinnate leaves. The winter-flowering variety of the Japanese cherry is a small tree, its bare branches decked all over with pale pink flakes of flower. It is a lovely sight against the sky, or in front of a dark background.

Descending to shrubs again, I should like to say a word in praise of Australian *Grevilleas*, and especially of the Rosemary-leaved one, which is seldom without its small clusters of red flowers all through the year. The one with yellow flowers [*juniperina* f. *sulphuria*] is tidier in habit and equally hardy, though not really so attractive. The Heaths need no commendation from me. The best here at Christmas time is that famous hybrid *Erica* x *darleyensis*, whose large round cushions are lilac-pink for months.

These seven plants were perhaps in a class by themselves at the end of December. But it would be wrong to differentiate too sharply. Here, for instance, are four others that may, in some years, run them close: *Rhododendron* 'Christmas Cheer', with its neat trusses of blush pink, followed by R. 'Nobleanum', one of the early hybrids made at the Knap Hill nursery over a hundred years ago, with trusses larger and of a bright rose colour: that modern buddleja from South Africa, B. *auriculata*, whose tiny flowers, delightfully fragrant, are set in grey calices and only reveal their pink-flushed tubes on close inspection; and the familiar *Berberis darwinii,* perhaps the most valuable of all the plants which the great Cornish collector, William Lobb, introduced from Chile just a century ago, with its polished evergreen leaves and its bright orange flowers in drooping racemes.

So much for the flowers – but we must not forget the berries. Of these none are better than the holly. I have a tall holly tree of which one trunk bears the well known shining green leaf and the other a very striking leaf variegated with cream, and both are well berried. No plant deserves to be treated with more respect than the holly: and it needs respectful treatment, for it is notoriously slow-growing. Yet rabbits bite off the bark when the tree is young, and when it is full grown it is butchered for the Christmas market. I should like to enlist every schoolboy in a corps for the protection of the holly. Christmas needs no other berries; but for varieties sake the garden offers a small selection. There were still a few translucent red berries on some of the *Berberis*, and similarly stray shining pink ones on the *Pernettya*. The Tasmanian creeper *Billiardiera* retains specimens of it beautiful cylindrical blue fruit, and there are yet tempting red strawberries on the *Cornus capitata*. These last are extremely attractive, but their insipid flavour is a great disappointment to the children who taste them.

Such treasure in the garden provides for our Christmas finery and decoration. A small earthenware pot on my wife's writing table was filled with three sprigs each of seven flowering shrubs, and charming and gay it looked. The choirmen's buttonholes this year included purple violets as well as Wintersweet, the heath and the cherry. Quite outstanding were certain unusual combinations: a sprig of the fragrant yellow *Mahonia* with three blue and yellow daisies of *Felicia amelloides*; three sprigs of the *Mahonia* with a cluster of pink *Pernettya* berries; a scented white *Camellia* with a cluster of the sweet, small, pink flowers of *Vallea stipularis*. I admit pride in the *Vallea*: it must be the only plant of this species in the West of England, and it has stood out two or three winters. But the first prize for buttonholes must certainly be given to one consisting of three pieces of Wintersweet and a red rosebud. The sweet engagement of summer and winter was completely lovely. Not surprising perhaps – but what did surprise me was the extraordinary charm of a head of the fragrant Winter Heliotrope (insidious intruder though it be) in a specimen glass with three bright yellow daisies and a leaf or two of soft fresh green on a spray of the open-air chrysanthemum.

Now in January we look not only to the future. There is treasure hidden in the garden, which can only be acquired at the cost of care and labour. So we have been taking thought for succeeding years and setting about a variety of tasks: cutting off the dead flower-heads of the *Hydrangeas* – blue-flowering *Hydrangeas* happily, as it is natural for them to be here in Cornwall; clearing off ivy and brambles from the old-established clump of Mollis Azaleas; giving the bed of *Rhododendron* x *praecox* more light and air by cutting off branches from overshadowing conifers; and checking Bamboos encroaching on a wide-spreading *Magnolia* x *soulangeana*. An ornamental crab on the front drive had long needed treatment. The wild apple which formed the root stock had forced its way upward and called attention to its success by a prodigal supply of worthless apples. Its tall, stout trunk took a great deal of getting down.

More exciting and more constructive was the planting out: of three Japanese *Skimmias* of distinctive quality; of a line of Golden Willows – a couple of dozen of them – which we had grown from cuttings taken from a tree I had long admired in a valley near Truro; of a *Kerria japonica*, not the ordinary double-flowered sort, but the rarer and more charming single-flowered; and of four *Malus hupehensis*. The last is a beautiful small tree from Western China, covered, when in full bloom, with a profusion of white pink-tinged blossoms. A place had also to be prepared, near the house and somewhat sheltered from the wind, for one of the best *Magnolias*. *Magnolias* from China find a home from home in Cornwall. We have grown several from our own seed; this winter I have sent a strong young *Magnolia wilsonii* to the churchyard of Mevagissey, the fishing village where my ancestors lived for several generations; and another to St. Clement's, on the banks of one of the reaches of the river Fal, where my grandmother was married. All gardeners love to see their plant-children properly set up for life.

So the New Year finds the garden full of hope for the years to come. But lest there should be exultation overmuch, I must in my last paragraph record a burglary. The burglars were bullfinches, or blue-tits, or both; and they have robbed my *Forsythia* of its buds. No sprays of golden flowers for me in the early spring. And it was the same last year. As the Gospel reminds us, there is no treasure on earth which thieves may not break through and steal.

(*The Guardian*, 27 January 1950, p. 46.)

The Buddleia Makes Amends

In July 1678 there entered St. Catherine's, Cambridge, a Lincolnshire boy who was to become, in his quiet way, one of the most accomplished botanists of his day. He was born at Deeping St. James, and his name was Adam Buddle. He became a Fellow of the college (1686–1691). As a non-juror he left Cambridge, though he subsequently conformed. For some time (1696–1698) he lived at Henley, in Suffolk, where some of his plants were collected and his two children were baptized. Among the short letters preserved in the Sloane collection of manuscripts in the British Museum is one addressed to James Petiver, an apothecary and botanist, one of Buddle's greatest friends, which begins, "To-morrow my child is to be made a Christian", and goes on to invite his friend to partake of a leg of pork.

Buddle was very fond of his friends and very hospitable. In another letter written on a Saturday about "3 of ye clock", he says: "Mr. Doody and I have pitched upon Monday to look over all ye familys of English plants, where ye will likewise meet with Mr. Stonestreet and a great leg of country pork and peas for dinner"; and in a postscript he adds, "My service to Mr. Airy whom I should be glad to see if his busyness would permit".

In the summer of 1699 Buddle and Petiver went together to visit "the Father of English Botany", "The incomparable Mr. Ray". John Ray was then living in a little house which he had built in his native village of Black Notley. Like Ray, Buddle had very limited means and, indeed, was sometimes on the verge of want. Thus, in one of his letters to Dr. Richardson, a wealthy friend in the North of England, who had made a great collection of rare plants, he writes: "I have not seen Mr. Woodward this half year, nor have I minded any thing of Botany, nor listened to anything of Naturall Philosophy, being too intent upon the necessities of life to think of the Nugae" [i.e. trifles].

In December 1702 Buddle was ordained priest at Ely, and shortly afterwards presented to the Crown living of North Fambridge in Essex. He also became Reader at Gray's Inn. How keenly he maintained his interest in Botany is shown by a letter to Dr. Richardson dated 13 June 1706:

> You used to talk of sending your grasses and mosses to me; and if you do not yet intend it, I do promise to fix their names and make what additions I can to them. My mind is as intent as ever: nay, I think my ardour rather increases; for having the compleating of my English collection always in view makes me passionately bent upon it, that I may live to see all our English plants hither-

to discovered; and I believe they are almost discovered.
My earnest and humble request to you is, that you would
send me fair specimens of all the rare northern plants
within your reach. Here is a delicate summer for the purpose; and, if there be any thing that I can serve you in,
pray command me.

The same year Buddle's friend, Samuel Doody, died at the age
of fifty. He was a great authority on mosses, but a hard drinker, and
he suffered severely from gout. On December 3 Buddle preached
his funeral sermon at Hampstead, and part of it is preserved in the
author's own handwriting in a manuscript in the British Museum.
He speaks in high terms of his friend, "a worthy member of ye
Royall society", and refers to Botany as "ye most innocent, most
primitive study designed at first even in paradise as a diversion for
ye busy inquisitive mind of Man".

Mosses and grasses were Buddle's specialities. Indeed, he was
known as "the top of the moss-croppers" and a botanical friend to
whom he lent his collection wrote on 4 April, 1707, to say: "I am
now to be thankfull to God and my Friends that I have not only
seen but had the perusall of (as I think) the best collection of its
kind in the World. I return y^r Book of Mosses wth as many thanks
as there are leaves among the said mosses".

By 1708 Buddle had produced a new English Flora in which he
claimed to have improved in some respects upon the methods of
previous botanists. The list of persons to whom he dedicated the
work is a very interesting one. It is headed by the most reverend
Father in God Bishop of Carlisle, and it includes the Rev. Mr.
Stonestreet (mentioned in his letter above), the Rev. Mr. Stephens
of Cornwall, Dr. Hans Sloane, a number of apothecaries, and two
gentleman farmers. The bishop was William Nicholson, at one time
a keen botanist and correspondent of Ray's, who referred to him at
an earlier period as, "an ingenious minister living in Cumberland".
He was, indeed, ingenious in more ways than one – but that is
another story. The Rev. Mr. Stephens is Lewis Stephens, born in
Devonshire, a scholar of Gonville and Caius College, Cambridge,
who transferred himself to Oxford and became a Fellow of Exeter
College. At the same time he took orders and was at once appointed Vicar of Treneglos and Warbstow, two parishes in the North of
Cornwall. These he resigned in 1685 when he was presented to the
important college living of Menheniot, also in Cornwall, which he

held till his death in 1715. He was known as a botanist, and some of the plants in Buddle's collection came from him.

In spite of these distinguished patrons, Buddle never succeeded in getting his book published. His manuscript, in not very legible handwriting, is still in the British Museum. None the less, his interest in botany was unabated. In a letter to Dr. Richardson dated from Gray's Inn 28 May, 1709, he sends grateful thanks for plants sent to him, both on his own account and on the account of his friends "to whom they were very acceptable: for I always distribute them as far as they will go" – here speaks the true gardener! "Botany", he goes on to say, "with all other branches of Naturall Philosophy, have for some years been at a stand: but I hope much from the ensuing peace" – the peace did not actually come for some years.

The concluding part of the letter shows that Buddle was taking a practical interest in the Apothecaries' garden at Chelsea: "You were pleased to say you would send me some seed and roots of your northern plants: they would be extreamly wellcome to me and to Chelsea Garden, which is now putting into good order; and in the first place we design (for I call myself of the number) to cultivate all the rare English plants we can get to grow there: and I hope you will answer our longing expectation of some from you, in answer to which I promise you the seeds or roots of any plants growing in the garden, which I assure you is very much improving".

The last of the short series of unpublished letters in the British Museum is a moving little note written by Mrs. Buddle, who is arranging to send her husband's collections and manuscripts to Dr. Hans Sloane –

> ... which I designe to do this day, for to my grate sorrow I find I must now lay aside all hopes of his recovery, My misfortune is such that I know not into whose hands they may fall if ye fatal hower is once past ... If you have any Books here I desire you will send for them while thay are in my power for God aloon know what I am to do or what to suffer, but am your distressed humble

sarvant
Eliz: Buddle

Wednesday evening
10 of ye clock

Poor lady – her husband died at Gray's Inn on 15 April, 1715, and was buried at St. Andrew's, Holborn, though no trace of his grave survives.

Buddle's herbarium is preserved in the Natural History Museum, South Kensington. It is contained in five handsome volumes in remarkably good condition. It is undoubtedly the most trustworthy and accurately named herbarium of the period. Sir Hans Sloane lent it to Dr. Dillenius who made use of it when he published his edition of Ray's *Synopsis Plantarum Britannicarum*, and also to Mr. Petiver who used some of the specimens for the illustrations in his English Herbal.

The work of Adam Buddle having thus been absorbed by others without adequate acknowledgement, it seemed as though his name would be forgotten except by a thin line of botanical specialists. But that is not the end of the story. Only a few years later (between 1730 and 1733) Dr. William Houston, who was much interested in botany and travelled in Central America collecting plants, named after Buddle one of his new genera. *Buddleia* he spelt it, though Linnaeus subsequently and mistakenly wrote Buddleja. Buddleia it must surely remain.

The original, type plant was *B. americana*. This, however is a dull plant; and there are many Buddleias brighter and better. In America they are popularly known as Butterfly Bushes, for their fragrant flowers are very attractive to butterflies. It is lovely to see a number of Red Admirals on the long purple sprays of a great *Buddleja davidii*, the commonest Buddleia in this country. This Buddleia is as resilient and generous as the good clergyman to whom it owes its name; and it is astonishing to see how gallantly it has striven on bombed sites to cast a veil of beauty over the scars of war. There are many other Buddleias of note, from various parts of the world: *B. globosa*, for instance, from Chile, with scented globe-flowers of tangerine orange; and a less satisfactory hybrid between the two. And here is Reginald Farrer's description of *B. alternifolia*, as he saw it in South Kansu in China: "It prefers steep dry banks and open warm places, where it grows like a fine-leaved and very graceful weeping willow, either as a bush or small trunked tree, until its pendulous sprays erupt all along into tight bunches of purple blossom at the end of May, so generous that the whole shrub turns into a soft and weeping cascade of colour". This Buddleia does well in many parts of England: and to mention but one more, the South African *B. auriculata* is in the South-west of England in bloom in the last week of November. The flowers are tiny, and grey in bud like a November day, but they are deliciously fragrant and exceedingly welcome.

How many gardeners to-day have heard of Dillenius or Petiver, or even of John Ray? But what gardener has not both seen and scented one or other of the great world-wide family named after that kind and modest, that assiduous and trustworty and un-rewarded, clergyman of the Church of England? The Buddleia has made amends.

(*The Guardian*, 31 March 1950, pp. 154–5.)

White Flowers for Easter

Easter Day cannot be earlier than March 22 or later than April 25. This year, therefore, Easter fell just in the middle of the possible period. Flowers accordingly were plentiful. The liturgical colour for Easter is everywhere white, the colour of light and purity and joy. Some people like white flowers best. My mother did, and my sister and I are specially glad to put white flowers on her grave on Easter Eve. This year it was white narcissus. Most of the narcissus were over, though the latest narcissus of all in my garden, a small white with a yellow eye and very fragrant, was still only in tight bud. There is no reason why flowers for Easter Day in church should all be white, though white and yellow will naturally, in accordance with long tradition, be the dominant note. And there is a wide range of choice. The sanctuary in Truro Cathedral on Easter morning had only Arum lilies and branches of *Magnolia*, and magnifical they looked: the lilies on stands on either side of the High Altar, and the magnolias grouped about the two large standing candles. Arum lilies have rather lost their vogue, but their solid whiteness is not out of place in a great church dedicated to Our Lady. The *Magnolia* was *M.* x *soulangeana*, with large white chalices flushed with purple. They are loveliest not quite fully open, and the tree in my garden was just perfect when I cut the branches on Easter Eve. The habit of this *Magnolia* (and of others) is to have branches criss-crossing in all directions, and to cut out some is no sacrifice but an improvement of the tree. I have a number of other species of *Magnolia* as small plants in various parts of the garden, but the only other large one is *M. stellata*. This must be one of the tallest of the species in England, and as it stands halfway up a little path it presents a great shield of white stars in March before its leaves appear. Cornwall is a good county for *Magnolias*, and nearly every year there are magnificent displays, beginning with the huge pink cups of *M. campbellii* (of which there is also a white form). One of the great sights at Caerhays at the end of March was *M. dawsoniana*, with hundreds of large pink flowers, though it is not actually one of my favourites. *M. salicifolia* with much smaller white flowers and fragrant bark and leaves, makes a lovely neat tree, which personally I much prefer. But the prize *Magnolia* in Cornwall this year was an unnamed variety[1] in the remarkable garden of Mr. Michael Williams at Lanarth in the Lizard peninsula. It was an astonishing sight in March, holding up about 250 lovely purple flowers against the sky. Mr. Williams put a few of the flowers in cold storage for the Cornwall Spring Show on March 28, and a specimen was exhibited in perfect condition, of a wonderful texture and colour – the most striking single object in the whole show.

I have strayed from the subject of white flowers for Easter, and I return to it by the delightful avenue of the white *Camellia*. In a box of primroses and polyanthus sent for Easter to St. Mark's Kennington, we put a few white *Camellias*. I have two large bushes of them in the garden, one has smaller and the other larger double flowers, all with rosettes of an exquisite whiteness and of a marvellous symmetrical pattern worthy of the Grand Geometrician of the Universe. At Caerhays there is a lovely hybrid called appropriately 'Cornish Snow', with charming white single flowers, not large but larger than those on the rare *Camellia sinensis*, which are slightly scented and deck the tall, thick shrub with delicacy and distinction.

Of the rhododendrons now flowering only a minority are white. I have three: one in the middle of a great clump of later rhododendrons. Its buds are flushed with pink, and it is pleasant to see it like a bouquet amid dark green leaves. Another white rhododendron is only just beginning to come out. Its plump trusses of bud are touched with pink, and the throat of the flower has purple markings. The third is a small plant, almost in full sun. It has grown but slowly, but it is covered with swelling buds of lovely creamy white.

Of the white heaths I have only one in flower. It is the tree heath, and it has been smothered with grey-white blossom for weeks. One of the best of the white heaths was intoduced to

England in the Caerhays garden. It was found in Southern Spain in 1912 by Robert, one of the sons of Mr. John Charles Williams, afterwards killed in the 1914–18 war. Robert brought it home to his father, who, naturally, prized it greatly. In the Caerhays garden book there is an entry dated April 8, 1918: "Bob's white *australis* is in flower well for the first time". Its full name is *Erica australis* 'Mr. Robert', and its flower clusters are rich and large.

Apart from cherries of various sorts, and pears now at the height of their white blossoming, other shrubs flowering white in the garden at the beginning of April are a broom, a spiraea, *Viburnum carlesii*, the Canadian Service-Berry (*Amelanchier*) and the Mexican Orange [*Choisya ternata*]. The broom is a native of Teneriffe [*Cytisus supranubius*]. My plants came fom Tresco, and I put them in one of my nursery beds. They grew luxuriantly and I forgot to move them. They are now too big to be transplanted: so these four children will have to remain in the nursery for the rest of their lives. From their thread-like branches, long racemes of white, slightly fragrant flowers have been hanging for weeks. The spiraea is *Spiraea* x *arguta*, one of the best spring-flowering shrubs for any garden. Mine is planted towards the back of a shrub border and put on its spring dress of little white star clusters so quickly that it was fully clad before I noticed it begin. *Viburnum carlesii* is here the most reliable of the scented *Viburnums*. Its large flower-clusters are pink-tipped in bud, of a clear white, and send out their delicious fragrance yards all round. Mine is grafted on stock of the native Wayfaring tree (*V. lantana*), and some gardeners maintain that so grafted it flowers more freely if the peristent suckers from the stock are rigorously cut off. The white flowers of my small tree of *Amelianchier* are fairy-like and fleeting. About Easter they were at their best. The Mexican Orange makes a tidy, rounded bush, and its blossom has a faint scent reminiscent of hawthorn. Easter is, of course, too early for the hawthorn itself: but the hedges in Cornwall are resplendent with the blackthorn. Against the black bark which gives its name to the shrub the tiny pure white flowers shine out gaily, braving the cold winds long before the leaf-buds dare unfurl their coverings. It was used with great effect on Easter Day in the ancient Church of Mylor on the West bank of Falmouth harbour. I had been there last autumn for Harvest Thanksgiving and had greatly admired the decorations then. "But you should see them at Easter" they said. I replied that I should very much like to, and then and there accepted the Vicar's kind invitation to preach in the evening of Easter Day. I preached to the Church and the Church to me. We had the same Resurrection. Primroses and daffodils set in fresh moss at the entrance to the choir: great branches of flowering cherries, white and pink: fine trusses of magnificent rhododendrons: bright anemones and soft green ferns – they were all far more eloquent of newness of life than I could hope to be. Behind the altar were two shining brass vases holding Arum lilies lightened with the more delicate whiteness of blackthorn and wands of white broom in bud; while north and south on the ledge above were two clusters of wide-open white daffodils with orange cups, looking down upon me like singing cherubs.

(*The Guardian*, 28 April 1950, p. 203.)

---

1 It has since been named *M. campbellii* ssp. *mollicomata* 'Lanarth'.

Cloven Tongues Like as of Fire

With cloven tongues like as of fire Pentecost divides both the Christian year and the year in the garden. This year the division is exactly halfway between Advent and Advent, and in the garden the cleft is similarly marked between spring and summer.

Cornish gardens are already past their prime. The elegant *Camellias*, most of the magnificent *Magnolias* and many of the *Rhododendrons* have the appearance of the morning after the ball. In Cornwall the great gardens have a flaming spring and a summer of quiet green. Now at the point of junction there is still no lack of red and white for Whitsun. As of fire are the fine bushes of Azaleas – 'Goldsworth Red' and 'Firebrand', and still more 'C.B. Van Nes', all flame-red. They are hybrids of *Rhododendron molle* and they grow equally well in the full sun or in half shade. A group of these Mollis Azaleas is one of the half dozen best things in the Bishop's garden at Truro. *Rhododendron calendulaceum*, the flame Azalea from the hills of Carolina, is brilliant itself and parent of such well known hybrids as 'Gloria Mundi' and 'Unique', of burning colour. With these for Whitsun decoration you may use a white Azalea: for instance *R. mucronatum*. I have a bush of it in a shady place in my garden, and this year it has covered itself in pure white flowers, slightly fragrant.

For the seventh time on the evening of Whitsunday I took confirmation in the parish church at Falmouth. There were over fifty candidates and a great congregation. The church was in its beautiful Whitsun array. The red-and-white effect was created largely by rhododendrons. In my own garden I have several reds, one of the very finest being, 'Fusilier', a cross made by Lord Rothschild in 1938. It is now coming into bloom. Of whites I have none at the moment pure white. 'Mrs. J.C. Williams' is white with a delicate light-brownish blotch: and 'Sappho' has stiff, upright trusses, white with dark purple eyes, which, as I sit on the lawn, look at me as in droll surprise.

The brightest white in my garden at the moment is that of *Viburnum* f. *tomentosum*. The white head of flower on one of my plants are round like snowballs: on the other ['Mariesii'] they are flat, whitening a wide spread of horizontal branches. I have also a few rather commonplace *Philadelphus*, generally known as "Syringa", with a very sweet scent. You seldom see a good "Syringa" in Cornwall. Of scented white flowers just now there is, of course, none to touch the lily-of-the-valley. My own are poor, but a friend presented us a week ago with a bunch of the largest and most fragrant I have ever seen, and it is lovely to see part of a woodland carpeted with them in the grounds of Ripon Hall, the Theological College on Boar's Hill near Oxford. In the long grass and shade at the back of my drive my only white is the white lace of cow parsley: but how charming it is and how effective in the hands of one who knows how to set up flowers!

The outstanding Whitsun flower at Falmouth is the South American Fire Bush, *Embothrium*. It has a wide range of habitat in Chile, at 3,000 to 5,000 feet in the hills and as far South as the Straits of Magellan; and there are several forms of it, some a good deal hardier than others. I am coaxing on three or four in my garden, but only one has yet reached the flowering stage and that but barely. Its great sprays of flower have an astonishing vivid redness, and I was delighted to see it again lighting up the sanctuary in Falmouth church. Yet, when all is said, the good red geranium is very hard to beat. The Rector of Falmouth showed me a plant in his cold greenhouse smothered with bright red blossoms, which he said had never been without flower since he brought it with him to Falmouth three years ago.

Another charming display of red flower is being given in my garden by a lantern tree from the Chilean forest, brought to England like the *Embothrium* by that remarkable Cornish plant-collector, William Lobb. It has more than one name, but none shorter than *Crinodendron hookerianum*, which is apparently, the name most favoured by the pundits at the present moment. It has dark green leaves with hanging lanterns of solid rose-crimson. The better of my two plants is the result of a cutting taken by my wife from a plant growing against the Vicarage at Charlestown near St Austell. It is easily propagated, either from seed or from cuttings, and it is one of the best large shrubs for the milder gardens. Yet another welcome red is provided by *Escallonia* 'C.F. Ball'. It is a vigorous hybrid having larger and brighter flowers than its parent *rubra* var. *macrantha*. *Macrantha*, with its shining gummy leaf, is one of the most familiar and useful of hedge plants for sheltering mild, windy gardens near the sea. A hedge of it was planted on Zennor Moor in an exposed position where there is no other bush bigger than gorse: and there *macrantha* has remained for fifty years, a solid ever-green windbreak 14 ft high. It is flowering at this moment in the Close on the north side of the cathedral, where draughts and dogs and small boys have so far defeated all my own efforts at planting. Happily the cathedral does not altogether lack flowers, for the City Council in the open space before the west front have planted a bed of those good red geraniums. There they were ready to usher in the great Feast of Whitsun. The only other red in my garden that calls for mention is that of the old red horse-chestnut. It has a hybrid where panicles of rose-coloured flowers have a great advantage that they are not followed by conkers. There are white horse-chestnuts in the churchyard behind my house which unfortunately attract an invasion of stone-throwing school-boys every autumn. How very slowly this country is learning to treat plants and trees with consideration and respect!

Onward now to summer – and the hedges will soon be lined with a guard of honour of red foxgloves as we approach Midsummer Day. An advance party has already posted itself in one of my borders, under the patronage, apparently, of members of the same family who claim a higher social standing by reason of their whiter colour and distinctive markings. Anyhow, I have no heart to expel them.

(*The Guardian*, 9 June 1950, p. 274.)

Shrubs of High Summer

In the first week of August I instituted a new rector to the parish of Creed. The parish church is beautifully situated by the river Fal, here just a rivulet before it falls into the long estuary leading through many windings eventually to Falmouth harbour. The Church – as not infrequently in Cornwall – is a mile from the centre of population, the old "rotten borough" of Grampound, once represented in Parliament by John Hampden. When I was a boy we used to make a pilgrimage to the churchyard once a year, as my mother's parents were buried there. I remember that the church was then in a poor state, but a little later it was lovingly restored. The squire refused to have stained glass put into the windows. He had always been accustomed to look out upon the fields and trees, and he wished always to do so.

Institutions are happy and popular occasions. The little church was full, and lovely it looked in the soft evening light. The white flowers in the chancel were in perfect harmony with their setting. They were white Hydrangeas of two kinds. The first *Hydrangea macrophylla* to be introduced into England, which caused a great sensation in 1789, has great rounded blooms consisting of pretty (sterile) florets. The white florets at Creed had pinpoints of blue at their centres. The other variety of *Hydrangea macrophylla* was collected in Japan by Charles Maries for the great firm of Veitch, and is called after him, 'Mariesii'. This form of *Hydrangea* has corymbs, i.e., flat clusters, with small fertile flowers in the centre and sterile florets in a ring outside. One of the best garden *Hydrangeas* of this sort is called 'Bluewave', and there is a fine healthy bush of it on the corner in my garden at Truro. Here in this acid soil, almost all my *Hydrangeas* are blue and retain their blueness year by year. I regularly cut out the dead wood each winter, and each summer they give me a rich reward for my friendly attention. But my collection of *Hydrangeas* is quite eclipsed by that at Trewithen, a lovely garden near Creed which I was visiting on the afternoon of the institution. There, great *Hydrangeas* of white and blue line paths in the light woodland, and they look so much more at their ease than their fashionable relatives in stiff tubs at the entrance of large hotels. One of the blues at Trewithen is very unusual and striking. I looked it up in the colour chart and decided that it was nearly, if not quite, *Capri blue*, a blue with green in it, very distinctive.

6   *Canon Boscawen with his* Eucryphia Nymansay *at Ludgvan Rectory.*

Under the woodland conditions at Trewithen I saw at its best that most beautiful white alder from Western China, *Clethra delavayi*: named after Delavay, the French missionary who discovered it in 1884. It has long white plumes of flower which stretch out in a more or less horizontal direction.

Here also was that lovely *Eucryphia* from South Chile, with flowers like a white St. John's Wort with a brush of yellow-topped stamens. It has a superb hybrid which formed itself in the gardens at Nymans in Sussex (*E.* x *nymanensis* 'Nymansay'). The best photograh I have of that great gardener, the late Canon Arthur Boscawen, shows him standing by the side of a plant of this *Eucryphia* in his rectory garden at Ludgvan, three times his height and covered with blossom. I planted one here a few years ago, and it has shot up like a tall mast, but it seems loathe to flower.

Another delightful plant blossoming freely at Trewithen was the tree myrtle (*Luma apiculata*), brought from Chile a hundred years ago by the Cornishman, William Lobb. It is fitting that the largest tree of it in England should be in the grounds of Scorrier House, near Redruth, where Lobb worked in the garden as a boy before he went to Chile. The leaves are small dark and decorative, the buds round like water-drops, and the multitude of little flowers have stamens touched with pink and a slight fragrance. The trunk is of a bright cinnamon-brown, very smooth, with pale patches where the bark has peeled off.

One plant in my own garden is unsurpassed, even at Trewithen. It is a *Hoheria* from New Zealand (*H. sexstylosa*) with its showering sprays all whitened with flower. I brought mine back as a little thing from Tresco in the Isles of Scilly and put it in my nursery at the top of my far garden. Here it grew with extraordinary rapidity, and before I had made up my mind where to put it it had become too big to move: and there it is still, a light graceful column of white. I have another species of Hoheria also, smaller but very elegant and very white with flower. They are my show-pieces in August.

One of my summer-flowering heaths has excelled itself this year. It is a garden variety of the Cornish heath [*Erica vagans*] known as 'Mrs. Maxwell', now a large cushion of warm-pink. It is a good year for *Ericas* in general. A whole hillside of purple heather at its brightest above the white breakers and blue sea at Porthtowan dazzled and delighted my eyes a week ago.

In this short article I am trying to limit myself to seven – seven shrubs of high summer – and I have been much exercised to choose from the numerous possibilities a seventh plant for my last remaining place. My *Hypericums* are not particularly good this year, though the tender one which I had from Tresco is becoming generously yellow; and a slender delicate plant with the smallest St. John's Wort buttercups I have ever seen is gay and charming. My *Fuchsias* are not doing themselves justice either. I do not mean the dolled up modern hybrids, smart and elegant as they are. I prefer my old friend from Edinburgh, the familiar *F. magellanica* with red calyx and purple petals, dangling from slender red stalks. It makes a fine windbreak near the sea and forms a delightful hedge, especially if cut down annually. But in my garden this is not the year for *Fuchsias*. My choice, after all, must fall on the Chinese Star-jasmine [*officinale*] climbing the wall outside my study. Never before has it been quite so lovely. For weeks its dark polished, evergreen leaves have been hidden by masses of white flowers. I can look through a chaplet of them at the spires of the cathedral a mile away in the valley below, backed by the blue waters of the estuary. They have filled my room with a delicious fragrance. In this kind enterprise they have received considerable assistance from a Japanese honey-suckle, yellow and white, round an adjoining corner. Not that the Japanese is better than the English honeysuckle of the hedgerows. Nothing could be better than the best of that, not the rich and vig-orous Mediterranean (*Lonicera etrusca*), or any other.

The window through which I see the Star-jasmine looks out into a little alcove on the south side of the house. I think of it as the bay of incense. For, mingling with the scent of jasmine and honeysuckle is the aromatic fragrance exuding from gum-Cistus and from scented-leaved pelargoniums, while the ancient *Magnolia grandiflora* on the wall adds an occasional white chalice of sweetness. Here, in ecclesiastical seclusion, the stoutest Protestant can exercise his olfactory abilities and give thanks for those odours of Edom which he scruples to enjoy in church.

(*The Guardian*, 18 August 1950, p. 395.)

Cambridge Gardens in the Long Vacation

Recent visitors to England are impressed by the tidying and bright-ening up which have taken place during the last year or two. Cambridge is a good example. Never have I seen the little garden round Great St. Mary's, the University Church, look so gay as it has been this summer with its masses of Polyantha Roses. And this new cheerfulness is typical of the whole University. A sumptuous account of "Oxford's College Gardens", with coloured illustra-tions, appeared nearly twenty years ago. I have never seen any parallel publication for Cambridge, and it has commonly been taken for granted that the Oxford gardens as a whole are the better. But if Cambridge continues to improve as it has been doing lately, the sister University will have to look to her laurels.

College gardens are hallowed by a long tradition. In one of the farewell letters written by Bishop Ridley at Oxford in October, 1555, just before his martyrdom, he refers to the garden of his old College, Pembroke, at Cambridge: "Farewell, Pembroke Hall", he writes, "of late mine own college, my cure and my charge! ... In thy orchard (the walls, butts and trees if they could speak, would bear me witness) I learned without book almost all Paul's epistles, yea and, I ween, all the canonical epistles, save only the Apocalypse. Of which study, although in time a great part did depart from me, yet the sweet smell thereof, I trust, I shall carry with me into heaven ..."

The only mention of any Cambridge college in all the writings of Sir Walter Scott occurs in *Woodstock*, where the two divines, Dr. Rochecliffe and the Presbyterian Nehemiah Holdenough meet each other in the guard-room as prisoners under sentence of death and exchange reminiscences of their college days at Caius. "The break-ing of the Principal's orchard so cleanly done", said the Doctor, "it was the first plot I ever framed, and much work I had to prevail on thee to go into it". "Oh, name not that iniquity", said Nehemiah. A couple of young apple trees now stand in what was the old President's garden, and there is a good crop of apples on one of them this year.

The long line of limes at Trinity down which Alfred Tennyson used to walk to see his friend Arthur Hallam has had to be cut down; but it has been replaced by a fine avenue of closely-planted young trees: limes again, naturally; but I expect *Tilia* 'Euchlora', rather than the common lime *T.* x *vulgaris*. The former, with darker glossy leaves, is free from attack by aphis, which makes the leaves sticky and black.

St. Catherine's ought somewhere to show prominently some good *Buddleja* in honour of the Rev. Adam Buddle, Fellow of the College (1686–1691), one of the greatest botanists of his day, after whom that fine family of free-flowering and hardy plants is named. I did not see any, and I have already ventured to offer to repair the omission.

The result in my own mind of a rapid and incomplete survey was to award the prize for college gardens in August, 1950, to Clare. Its stately and gracious main building and its charming situation on the river give the college an initial advantage of which full use has been made; and its herbaceous borders, with their harmonious and glowing colours, are full of sunshine and delight. Other colleges have bright and beautiful herbaceous borders too; and everywhere this year – owing, no doubt, to the abundance of rain, the grass lawns, so well kept in every College, are of a soft fresh green. I noted with special pleasure the racemes of rosy pink upon a *Robinia* on the west-facing wall of the Great Court of Trinity; and the flourishing mulberry in the garden of Sidney Sussex, with the grass underneath thickly strewn with fruit. It is evidently a good year for mulberries, for my own at Truro has also borne abundantly. I was glad to see at Girton the pretty leaves of the shrubby germander (*Teucrium fruticans*), some healthy young plants of Farrer's *Buddleja* (*alternifolia*), and a well-grown Judas Tree [*Cercis siliquastrum*]; though in May the bright rosy-purple flowers on the bare branches of this last must swear violently against the hot red brick of the college walls. But, as a gardener eager to learn, it was, naturally, from the University Botanic Garden that I gained most of all. The Cambridge garden is a well-laid out piece of ground occupying about twenty acres on the south side of the town; and, divesting myself as far as I possibly can of the prejudices of piety, I think it would generally be granted that it is of far greater botanical interest than the older and more famous five-acre Physick Garden at Oxford, charming as that is.

It is very pleasant to be caught doing the right thing, and as I was going round the garden with the Guide written by my friend, the Director, open in my hand, he overtook me and clapped me on the shoulder – to my very great advantage, for he was able quickly to draw my attention to what were the things most worth seeing at the moment. I had already admired a hibiscus with flowers of a rich blue, the small hard green oranges on the Chinese *Poncirus trifoliata* in a sunny sheltered position outside the Fern House, the dainty white racemes on a fine hybrid catalpa with lustrous light green leaves, and the silky wigs on the Venetian Sumach [*Cotinus coggygria*]. The Director showed me, the rather tender *Abelia schumannii* against a wall in good flower of rosy pink, one of the handsomest of abelias. I myself have only *A. grandiflora,* less pink, but hardier and of graceful habit. I asked about his great clump of *Garrya elliptica*. The green catkins already forming looked as though they would never be so long as those we see in Cornwall, and he said that was so. I had been looking at the tall *Xanthoceras sorbifolia* outside the Superintendent's house, probably the largest in the county. Its beautiful white flowers are produced in May and were, of course, over. But the tree has a special interest for me because I had just been reading the travel diary of that intrepid French missionary priest in China, l'Abbé David, and had noted an entry dated May 31, 1866: "To-day I also find for the first time in its wild state the handsome *Xanthocera sorbifolia* cultivated in Pekin as an ornamental tree, of which I have just sent plants to the Paris Museum".

For the first time I saw the Tree of Heaven (*Ailanthus altissima*) in full fruit. The fruit consists of keys like those of the ash. They are borne in hundreds on large branching panicles and are a reddish brown in colour. The total effect is extremely handsome. But most splendid of all sights I saw that day was the Chinese Golden Rain Tree (*Koelreuteria paniculata*). It was a fine great shapely tree, blazing with a mass of deep yellow flowers. It is named after J.G. Koelreuter, a professor at Karlsruhe in the eighteenth century, and no man could have a lovelier namesake.

(*The Guardian*, 15 September 1950, p. 442.)

The Year Fades Out

The gardening year and the Christian year grow old and fade together. In the charming little books which give pictures of trees and shrubs flowering throughout the year, the lists are at their shortest in November. By the end of the month Nature, in this temperate zone, has sunk to that short slumber which is all she takes. Here in Cornwall fading is the right word. There is very little of the flaring up of autumn colour which surprises and delights the drier parts of England, where, though the winter is much colder, the sun is much hotter in the summer. Here the leaves from the lime and the beech and the elm fall a dull brown. One week the whole tree appears a fading yellowish-green, then perhaps comes a storm of wind, and the next week the tree displays the beautiful tracery of its bare branches. There is nothing between.

With us there are a number of shrubs which find great difficulty in deciding whether to shed their leaves or not; that wonderful fire-bush from Chile the *Embothrium* is an example, the hardy narrow-leaved form being the most deciduous. The Strawberry Tree from the Himalayas, commonly called Benthamia [*Cornus capitata*], though supposed to be deciduous, keeps most of its green leaves throughout the winter in gardens like mine. Its great flattish strawberries ripen red deliciously, and are regarded as a delicacy in China. We find them insipid or unpleasant. Perhaps in the Chinese climate they acquire a different flavour. The other species of Strawberry Tree, the *Arbutus* [*unedo*], which is a native woodland tree in the South West of Ireland, has smaller, rounder berries, which, among its dark leaves, are a charming decoration for Christmas. Even lovelier is the Californian *Arbutus* [*menziesii*] with bunches of orange fruit deepening to vermilion. It does well in the South of England.

Birds and Berries

But after all, is there any berrying tree more bright and beautiful than our own holly, with its glossy leaves and shining red berries, or than the Mountain Ash, loaded so generously with large clusters of scarlet? Unfortunately the birds are fond of both, and this year they have been stripping the branches very early. Birds are increasing in and around my garden. I wonder why. Partly, I suppose, because of the mildness of the last two winters in the West, and partly because so many woods have of late been thinned and stripped. Happily, the birds have not yet found my *Pernettyas*, though no doubt they will when other food becomes scarce. My plants are loaded with little solid plums of a delicate purplish pink. More happily still, my clump of that fine berrying *Viburnum, V. betulifolium*, has at last given an earnest of those cascades of translucent scarlet berries which birds do not touch. Less conspicuous, but more unexpected and distinguished, are the oblong, deep blue fruits on the slender Tasmanian climber (*Billardiera*) on my study wall. Nor must I forget to mention the waxy berries like tiny red candle-sticks which lighten so prettily the dark needles of my tallest Yew, and make it a giant Christmas Tree.

My best berrying Cotoneaster this year is *C. lacteus*, which is just a mass of charming coral. The Fire-thorn (*Pyracantha*), over the kitchen door, is orange-scarlet with berries at the top where it gets most sun. Sunshine, too, has made all the difference as regards autumn colouring between my two *Forsythias*. It is only the one out of the shade that has turned a burnished red. This, with the cheerful yellow of a spreading Maple, provides the little colour that I have, except, indeed, for those most rewarding plants Azaleas, especially the common yellow one [*luteum*], which not only smothers itself with fragrant honeysuckle flowers in the spring, but flames with vivid foliage in the autumn.

After the Summer

My *Hydrangeas* deserve a sentence all to themselves for they hold their huge blue heads of flower for so long, and then fade into an astonishing tapestry green, in which state they are extremely decorative and lasting.

I spoke of sunshine, but Cornwall has not for many years had so grey and damp a summer, and though the visitors have found it trying, the shrubs have enjoyed it, and so have the weeds. I have resolved on a campaign of tidying. Now is the opportunity: as the year dies down, the weeds die down too. And by the beginning of December the garden, with short grass and brown earth and re-planted borders, will look tidier and barer than at any other period of the year.

It will look bare and at rest. But what is going on beneath the surface, underground? Vast preparations for the advent of the new year that comes silently in as the old year passes silently out.

Some of the preparations have been going on for a very long time indeed. The bloom of the daffodil which will expand early next spring, was formed as long ago as last May, the flowers of the snowdrop and the crocus were beginning to be developed last June, the "lamb's-tails" on the filberts were already being formed in July. Now, in this mild November the little fat flower buds are swelling on the *Rhododendrons*: yellow on *R.* x *praecox*, bright green on that famous beauty the 'Countess of Haddington', and red, picked out with white, on 'Lady Alice Fitzwilliam'.

"Hail and Farewell"

Thus it must be "hail" and "farewell". We must find a wreath for the old year and a bouquet for the new, the wreath of flowers just going over and the bouquet of flowers just coming on. The first will be a patch-work of bits and pieces, roses, and pinks, yellow Japanese Honeysuckle, delicate dangling *Fuchsias*, a lavender spray or two of *Hebe*, a nodding orange cup of *Abutilon*, a sprig of bright yellow *Hypericum*, a whitish head of *Ageratina*, fragrant incense, the strange large reddish trumpets of the procrastinating *Brugmansia*, and the little rosy pink spikes of *Polygonum vaciniifolium*, which has been gay for months on end.

There will be less variety in the bouquet: that dear old standby Laurustinus, the cool lilac-pink of *Erica* x *darleyensis*, a twig of the winter-flowering *Prunus*, bright with tiny semi-double stemless flowers, flushed white, 'Princess of Wales' violets, deliciously scented both in flower and leaf, and an early blush-pink truss of *Rhododendron* 'Christmas Cheer'.

(*The Cornish Guardian and Gazette*, 9 November 1950.)

Bibliography

Bishop Hunkin's horticultural writings – his theological and other works are not included here – appeared principally in the *Journal of the Royal Horticultural Society* (JRHS) and *The Guardian*, although two were also contributed to the *Gardeners' Chronicle*. They are arranged below in chronological order, items without specific dates being listed at the end of the entries for that particular year. Brief descriptive notes have been added regarding the contents and importance of some of the articles.

1942   'William and Thomas Lobb: Two Cornish Plant Collectors', *JRHS*, 1942, pp. 48–51.

> In this article, which rehabilitates the memory of these two great plant collectors for Veitch's nursery, Bishop Hunkin announced his intention of raising funds to erect a tablet commemorating the brothers in Devoran church, where Thomas was buried. See further under 1947 below.

'Arthur Townshend Boscawen, Parson and Gardener', *Journal of the Royal Institution of Cornwall*, 1942, pp. 1–24, 3 plates.

> An extended appreciation of Canon Boscawen (1862–1939) and his rectory garden at Ludgvan. The Bishop was President of the Royal Institution of Cornwall (RIC) at the time of writing.

1943   'John Charles Williams', *JRHS*, 1943, pp. 9–18, 2 plates; pp. 43–8, 2 plates.

> An appreciation of the great Cornish gardener, of Caerhays Castle and Werrington Park. The article makes considerable use of the unpublished 'Caerhays Garden Book', begun in 1897, as well as printed articles by J.C. Williams (1861–1939).

1943–50   The *Guardian* articles: 39 articles were published from 19 February 1943 to 15 September 1950. The dates and page numbers have been printed at the foot of each of the articles. A fortieth article was published posthumously in *The Cornish Guardian and Gazette* on 9 November 1950, for which see below.

'A Hundred Years of Cornish Gardening (1840–1940), with special reference to flowering trees and shrubs', *JRHS*, 1943, pp. 260–268; pp. 296–304.

> (*Lecture given on 8 June 1943, Major A.A. Dorrien-Smith in the Chair.*) The article describes 24 major gardens, and is followed by a select bibliography. It constitutes the only substantial survey of Cornish gardens between those of Edgar Thurston in his *Trees and Shrubs of Cornwall* (1930) and Patrick Synge in Volume 1 of the *Gardens of Britain* series (1977) for the RHS, which has been followed in more recent years by a proliferation of 'Garden Guides'.

1944   '*Furcraea Longaeva* at Tresco in the Isles of Scilly', *JRHS*, 1944, pp. 355–6.

1945   'Who was John Hollybush?', *JRHS*, pp. 19–20.

'The Making of Lanarth', *JRHS*, pp. 63–72, 2 plates; pp. 104–10, 8 plates; pp. 132–5.

> The articles open with an extract from the genealogical table of the well-known gardening family of Williams, and continue with an extensive survey of the unpublished 'Garden Book'. This is the fullest printed record of a once notable garden created by Percival Dacres Williams VMH (1865–1935), cousin of John Charles at Caerhays.

1946   'Pencarrow a Hundred Years Ago', *JRHS*, 1946, pp. 364–9, 1 plate.

> The article is followed by a 'Bibliography'. As in his previous articles on J.C. and P.D. Williams, the Bishop here describes another historic 'Garden Book' – *Trees planted by Sir William Molesworth, Bart., from 1833–1853*, with a supplement by his successor Mrs Mary Ford, checked in 1902, and again by Bruce Jackson in 1927–8.

Trees and Shrubs for Cornwall – Some Suggestions, published by The Council for the Preservation of Rural England (Cornwall Branch) and the Royal Horticultural Society ... London. Undated, but probably late 1946 or early 1947, pp. 48, 8 plates.

> In 1944 W. Arnold-Forster had been invited by the Cornwall branch of the CPRE 'to prepare a book on the Planting of Trees and Shrubs in Cornwall ... His labours, however, were interrupted by important national service'; consequently Bishop Hunkin was requested to produce an interim booklet. This begins with suggestions for trees and shrubs in various habitats, followed by an alphabetical list of plants with advice on planting. It concludes with seasonal selections – 'The Circling Year' – and a bibliography, the latest entry being dated March 1946. Arnold-Forster's *Shrubs for the Milder Counties* was published by *Country Life* in 1948; a new edition, with a new introduction, an addendum of plant name changes, and colour photographs was published by Alison Hodge in 2000.

1947   'Open-air Flowers at Tresco on New Year's Day', *Gardeners' Chronicle*, 1947, i., pp. 43–4.

'A Further Note on the Brothers William and Thomas Lobb', *JRHS*, 1947, pp. 33–5.

> Contains additional information on the Lobbs, most notably in relation to Curtis's *Botanical Magazine*, where William was found by the Bishop to have been associated 'with no fewer than a hundred of the plants figured, and Thomas with sixty-one,' to which references are given. The proposed tablet in Devoran church was unveiled by Lord Clifden on Friday, 2 October 1942, and four Lobb introductions planted in the churchyard. Four more were planted at Egloshayle, Wadebridge, where it was discovered that the brothers had been baptised.

'Tresco under three reigns. Part I – Augustus Smith, M.P., Lord Proprietor of the Isles of Scilly, 1834–1872; and Thomas Algernon Dorrien-Smith, 1872–1918', *JRHS*, 1947, pp. 177–91, 4 plates; 'Part II. Tresco under Major Arthur Dorrien-Smith', *JRHS*, 1947, pp. 221–37, 6 plates.

> These two articles, besides containing references to original documents and privately printed material, include references to all the

Tresco plants mentioned in Curtis's *Botanical Magazine*, and conclude with a full 'Bibliography'. It was the most comprehensive survey up to that time, which formed the unacknowledged source for Ronald King's account of the garden in his book, *Tresco England's Island of Flowers* (1985).

'The centenary of three introductions of distinction', *JRHS*, 1947, pp. 485–6, 2 plates.

> The three plants – '*Ceanothus rigidus* var. *pallens* ... *Philesia buxifolia* ... and *Lapageria rosea*', had been introduced by William Lobb.

'Bright Flowers at Tresco in mid-September', *Gardeners' Chronicle*, 1947, ii, p. 118.

> A sequel (after the 'great frost') to the previous article written at the beginning of the year. This may be compared with a similar article in *The Guardian* on page 74 above with the title 'Recovery'.

'The Gardens of Tresco', in E.A.Belcher, *The Isles of Scilly*, Footpath Guides no. 4, 1947, Ch. 4, pp. 33–59, 2 plates.

> Includes a tour of the garden.

1948 'Some of the Shrubs of Scilly', *Scillonian*, March 1948, pp. 81–4.

'Some Notable Plants in Cornish Gardens', *JRHS*, 1948, pp. 201–10, 12 plates.

> (*Lecture given on 20 April 1948*, Col. F.C. STERN, F.L.S., V.M.H., in the Chair.)

1949 'The Garden at Tresco', *Endeavour*, July 1949, pp. 125–9.

1950 'Ninety Years a Gardener – Captain W.S.C. Pinwill of Trehane', *JRHS*, 1950, pp. 326–31.

> Capt. Pinwill (1831–1926) inherited Trehane in 1861 and was awarded the VMH by the RHS in 1915. Bishop Hunkin regarded 'the succession of great Cornish gardeners' as beginning with the Hon. John Townshend Boscawen, Rector of Lamorran, followed by Capt. W. Stackhouse C. Pinwill, and then passing to J.C. and P.D. Williams.

'*Euonymus pendulus*', *JRHS*, 1950, p. 362.

'The Year Fades Out', *The Cornish Guardian and Gazette*, 9 November, 1950.

> At the foot of the article, there followed the note – '[This article is published with and courtesy of the church weekly paper, "The Guardian," to which Dr. Hunkin was a frequent contributor. – Editor.]'

1951   'South American Shrubs for the South-West', *Doige's Western Counties Annual*, 1951, pp. 108–11, 1 plate.

> 'Specially contributed by the Lord Bishop of Truro (J.W. Hunkin, M.C., D.D.)' The illustration was of the Bishop with his gardener, W.T. Blakey (see above, page 15). The article was printed before the Bishop's death at the end of October 1950.

Plants in Lis Escop Garden

It is providential that Bishop Hunkin's list of plants, together with a plan of their positions in the garden, has been preserved in the Diocesan Office, which now occupies an annexe built in the grounds when Lis Escop was used as the Cathedral School, to whom I am indebted for the copy used here. The plants are numbered 1–207, to correspond with their entries on the plan, and they are arranged in sections headed with directions for a tour of the garden. The list is undated, but since it omits plants described as lost in the great frost of 1947, and does not include several plants described in the *Guardian* articles after 1948, it was probably compiled between those dates. This receives some confirmation in one of these articles, published on 24 December 1947, in which the Bishop describes a seventeenth-century manuscript in Magdalen College, Oxford, written by a Fellow, the Revd Walter Stonehouse, in which he had described his rectory garden at Darfield in the West Riding of Yorkshire, with a plan (see page 80). This manuscript, printed in the *Gardeners' Chronicle* in May 1920, may well have been the inspiration for Bishop Hunkin to follow his example.

The list appears to have been a fair copy, rather than a working document, since there are almost no alterations, save for 39 deletions, not always of especially tender plants. It seems possible that these crossings out may have been made after Bishop Hunkin's death, by someone, perhaps his gardener, checking which of his plants were still surviving.

My initial reaction when first reading through this list was one of *déjà vu*, since, even though it included many unusual plants, there was an air of familiarity about it. The reason soon became clear when I noticed that Bishop Hunkin had obtained many of his plants either from Marchant's nursery in Wimborne, Dorset, which at that time had one of the most comprehensive collections of unusual shrubs and trees in the country, or else from Tresco Abbey Garden. This had been exactly the practice of my predecessor at

Gulval Vicarage, near Penzance over the same period, who was described by the Bishop himself in one of his *Guardian* articles as 'a keen gardener'.

In the following list I have arranged the plants alphabetically, with the numbers of the pages where they are mentioned in the *Guardian* articles as being in Lis Escop garden. This has provided the opportunity for incorporating those other plants which either had been lost before the list was compiled, or obtained later, in many cases adding the species names where these had been omitted. All of these additions have been enclosed in round brackets.

As was explained in the Introduction, it is impossible to avoid the necessity of bringing the botanic names up to date, even though many of my generation will find this tiresome. However, I have taken the opportunity, where there seems no question, to identify more precisely some of those plants which have not been fully named. These emendations have beeen placed in square brackets.

Abelia (*grandiflora*), 53, 114, 134

Abutilon pictum 'Thomsonii', 52, 114, 137

Abutilon vitifolium x 4, 60

(*Acacia baileyana*, 'under glass'), 26, 43

(Acacia [dealbata?]), 62, 77

Acacia paradoxa

Acer, *136*

Aesculus californica,

(*Aesculus* x *carnea*), 128

(*Ageratina ligustrina*), 53, 60, 113, 115, 137

Akebia (*quinata*), 73

Aloysia triphylla

(*Amelanchier canadensis*), 125

(*Amaryllis belladonna*), 114

Armeria [*maritima*] var., 87

Azalea x 2, 95

Azalea Mollis x 2, 44, 85, 117, 126

Azara x 3,

Azara dentata, 86

Azara microphylla

(Bamboo), 52, 95, 118

Berberis x 2, 117

Berberis beaniana

Berberis darwinii, 116

Berberis francisci-ferdinandii

Berberis lycioides

Berberis wilsoniae 'Comet'

(*Billardiera* [*longiflora*]), 114, 117, 136

Brachyglottis 'Sunshine'

Bruckenthalia spiculifolia

Brugmansia [*sanguinea*], 52, 93, 97, 137

Buddleja x 3, 113

Buddleja alterniflora, 92

Buddleja auriculata, 52, 116

Buddleja globosa, 113

Buddleja stenostachya

Calceolaria integrifolia, 40

Callicarpa bodinieri var. *giraldii* x 2

Camellia japonica 'Speciosa' x 3, 52
Camellia oleifera x 2, 37, 52, 116
Camellia (deep pink), 63, 97
Camellia reticulata
Camellia (white) 3 vars., 124
(*Campsis radicans*), 114
Carpenteria californica
Caryopteris x *clandonensis*, 113
Cassinia fulvida, 53
Ceanothus
Ceanothus papillosum ssp. *roweanus*
Cedrus libani ssp. *atlantica* 'Glauca'
Celastrus orbiculatus, 108
Ceratostigma willmottianum, 40
Chaenomeles speciosa
Chimonanthus praecox, 25, 43, 51, 93, 115
Choisya ternata x 2, 86, 125
(*Chrysanthemum*, 'single'), 93
Cistus x 5, 77, 88
(*Cistus* [*ladinifer*]), 132
Clematis
Clerodendron x 5
Clethra delavayi
Clianthus puniceus x 2, 74
(*Colutea arborescens*), 115
(*Convallaria majalis*), 127
(*Convolvulus sebatius*), 74, 93, 108, 112
Cornus capitata, 117, 135
Cornus florida f. *rubra*, 37, 97
(*Coronilla valentina* ssp. *glauca*), 52
Correa (yellow), 52, 76
Correa 'Carnea', 52, 76
Corylopsis sinensis var. *sinensis*
(*Corylus avellana*), 115
Cotoneaster
Cotoneaster lacteus, 136
(*Crassulas*), 62
Crinodendron hookerianum, 128
Cytisus, 88

(*Cytisus supranubius*), 125

Daphne odora, 25, 63, 96
Daphne odora f. *marginata*
Desfontainia spinosa
Deutzia
Dianthus, 137
Dianthus 'Mrs Sinkins', 87

Embothrium coccineum, 127, 135
(*Epilobium canum* ssp. *canum*), 113
Erica x 2, 51, 63
(*Erica vagans* 'Mrs Maxwell'), 131
Erica x *darleyensis*, 26, 96, 116, 137
Erica ('tree heath' [*australis*]), 52, 124
Escallonia ('Donard Gem'), 38, 95
Escallonia 'P.C. Ball', 95, 128
Escallonia ('Slieve Donard'), 38, 95
(*Eucalyptus*), 62, 77
Eucryphia (x *nymanensis*), 130
Eurya japonica

(*Felicia amelloides*), 117
Ficus carica 'Brown Turkey', 59
(*Forsythia* [x *intermedia* 'Spectabilis']), 99, 118, 136
Fremontodendron mexicanum
Fuchsia x 2, 52, 93, 113, 131, 137
(*Fuchsia* 'Beauty of Exeter'?), 93
Fuchsia ('creeper')
(*Fuchsia magellanica*), 131
Fuchsia recurva [?] x 2

Garrya elliptica, 53, 134
Genista, 52
Genista hispanica x 2
Grevillea juniperina f. *sulphurea*, 97, 116
Grevillea rosmarinifolia, 52, 97, 116
Griselinia [*littoralis*], 77

Bishop Hunkin's Memorial Plants

In one of the *Guardian* articles on the rectory garden at Bitton, Bishop Hunkin quoted Canon Ellacombe's 'favorite doctrine ... that a true gardener is known by the pleasure he takes in giving young plants to his friends.' In a later article, he wrote himself of his own 'little nursery where I am bringing on plants for my friends.' By then he had already begun his imaginative plan for donating plants from Lis Escop to every churchyard throughout the diocese, but at the time of his tragic and sudden death a year later he had been able to supply only a few parishes, although eventually 52 – about a quarter of the total – were to receive plants.

After his death many, led by his friend and mentor W. Arnold-Forster of Eagles' Nest (a house perched on a crag on the north coast near St Ives), who had succeeded him as chairman of the Cornwall branch of the CPRE, decided that they should 'carry the Bishop's scheme to completion, as [their] contribution to the county's memorial to him.' Consequently they at once sought the advice of incumbents, so that by the end of April 1951 'the task was finished'. Some of the plants were purchased by the CPRE itself; some were distributed from the small stock at Lis Escop (JWH), and others were given from gardens throughout the county. Arnold-Forster (AF) himself took the lead, supplying wind-hardy shrubs to the more exposed churchyards. He was joined by Dorrien Smith (DS) from Tresco, George Johnstone (GT) from Trewithen, Treve Holman from Chyverton, and several others, including Miss Waterer, who contibuted a *Eupatorium* from 'Eden Valley', her remarkable garden in Ludgvan.

A typed schedule of the completed Memorial resides in the Record Office (reference DDX 524/103), which is reproduced here with the permission of the County Archivist. No attempt has been made to fill out, or update the plant names, other than to print the botanic names in italics, and place the cultivar names between single quotation marks. The names of the donors follow the plant names, using the initials within brackets already noted – all the rest being purchased.

There remains the question – where are the plants today? My own – at present limited – rambles through churchyards have so far turned up no great number. Why should this be? My experience may be a case in point. I came from London to Gulval as vicar in 1961, to a parish which, except perhaps for St Just in Roseland, has the most picturesque churchyard in Cornwall, maintained at that time by a sexton/gardener. And yet, even though only ten years later, there was no sign of the *Magnolia campbellii* or the *Clethra arborea* which are recorded as having been donated. Nor, moreover, was I ever informed either by my church officials or parishioners that any such a gift had been made. Indeed, I never heard of the Memorial scheme itself until after I had left the diocese and began taking an interest in garden history. Such is the shortness of people's memories!

But this does not mean that in general the Memorial has been entirely forgotten. It aroused great interest and enthusiasm at the time, and many of the older generation still recollect and enquire after it, which is justification for reproducing the schedule here. However, it must be recognised that most – probably all – of the plants were small from nurseries, and thus especially susceptible to the ravages of time and weather, if not sometimes of lack of interest or simple neglect. The magnificent *Magnolias* and *Davidias* which might have graced churchyards throughout the county, in retrospect are seen to have required much more loving care and attention as young plants than perhaps could be expected in the average churchyard. It has been the camellias and rhododendrons on the whole that have proved tough enough to survive against the odds.

Nonetheless it is hoped that the following record of this remarkable and innovative scheme will, on it own, form a fitting conclusion to a book which is itself a memorial to Bishop Hunkin's love, not only of plants, but also of his native Cornwall.

S. Agnes	*Hamamelis mollis*	**Botus Fleming**	*Rh.* 'Lady A. Fitzwilliam' (JWH)
S. Allen	*Magnolia mollicomata* Wintersweet (JWH)	**Boyton**	*Rh.* 'Betty Wormald'
Altarnun Bolventor	Judas Tree 2 *Pyracantha*	**Breage**	*Cornus capitata* (JWH) *Olearias* (DS)
Antony	*Pyracantha* *Hoheria* (DS)	**Germoe**	*Hoheria*, *Drimys* (AF) *Crinodendron* (AF) Red Willows (JWH)
S. John	*Camellia* (JWH) *Davidia* (GJ)		
S. Austell	*Camellia* (more to follow)	**S. Breoke, Wadebridge**	*Camellia* (Holman)
Baldhu	*Hoheria* (DS) Tree Myrtles (AF)	**Bude**	Judas Tree
S. Blazey	*Camellia*	**Budock**	2 *Hoherias* (DS) 2 *Hydrangeas*
Blisland Temple	*Chaenomeles* *Senecio, Olearia* (AF)	**S. Buryan**	3 *Olearia macrodonta major* 2 *Hydrangea* 'Goliath'
Boconnoc Bradoc	*Camellia* 4 *Hydrangeas* 4 *Azaleas* (Martyn)	**Calstock**	*Camellia*
Bodmin	*Camellia* *Hoheria* (DS)	**Camborne**	*Camellia williamsii* (JWH)
Helland	2 *Azaleas* (Martyn)	**Carbis Bay**	*Pittosporum tobira*
Nanstallon	2 *Eupatorium* (Miss Waterer)		

Cardynham	*Camellia williamsii* and Red Willows (JWH)	**S. Columb Major**	2 *Rosa moyesii* (JWH) 2 *Azaleas* (Martyn) *Chaenomeles*
Carnmenellis	*Hebe dieffenbachii* (D. Thomas) *Senecios* (AF)	**S. Columb Minor**	*Pieris japonica*
Pencoys	*H. dieffenbachii* (D. Thomas) *Senecios* (AF)	**Constantine**	*Camellia*
Porkellis	*Escallonia* 'Apple Blossom' (D. Thomas)	**Crantock**	not wanted
		Creed	*Cornus capitata* (JWH) *Rh.* 'Lady A. Fitzwilliam' (JWH)
Chacewater	*Eucryphia nymansensis*		
Charlestown	*Rh.* 'Lady A. Fitzwilliam' (JWH) *Escallonia* 'Iveyi' (JWH)	**Crowan**	Holly 2 *Davidias* (GJ)
		Cubert	not ready
S. Cleer	*Chaenomeles*	**Cury Gunwalloe**	*Olearias* (AF) *Senecios* (AF)
S. Clement	*Magnolia mollicomata* (JWH) *Camellia* *Drimys*	**Davidstowe**	*Rh.* 'Purple Splendour' *Rh. ponticum* (Mrs Ball)
S. Clether	*Berberis* 'Flame'	**Otterham**	*Cornus capitata* (JWH) 3 *Azaleas* (Martyn) *Davidia* (GJ) *Hoheria* (DS)
Colan	*Magnolia* x *soulangiana* 'Alexandrina' *Davidia, Drimys* (GJ) 2 *Cupressus* *Hoheria* (Martyn)	**S. Day**	*Camellia williamsii* (JWH)

S. Dennis	*Chaenomeles* *Pyracantha*	**S. Eval**	3 *Olearia* *macrodonta* *major.* Senecios (AF)
Devoran	previously supplied	**Mawgan in Pydar**	*Camellia* *Davidii* (GJ)
S. Dominic	Tulip Tree	**S. Ewe**	*Camellia*
Duloe	*Arbutus* *Cornus, Hoheria* (JWH)	**Falmouth King Charles**	*Embothrium* 'Norquinco' *Pittosporum*
Herodsfoot	*Chaenomeles* Tree Myrtle (AF)		*eugenioides* variegated
S. Pinnock	*Magnolia* *rostrata* (JWH) *Davidia* (GJ)	**All Souls**	*Magnolia stellata*
		S. Feock	*Camellia* *williamsii* (JWH)
Egloshayle	*Rh.* 'Lady A. Fitzwilliam' (JWH)	**Flushing**	*Magnolia* *grandiflora* (DT)
Egloskerry	White Lilac, *Rosa moyesii* (JWH)	**Forrabury**	*Senecios* and *Olearias*
S. Endellion	*Senecios, Olearias, Hydrangeas* (AF)	**Trevalga Minster**	(AF)
S. Enoder	*Crinodendron*	**Fowey**	*Malus* 'Lemoinei'
S. Erme	*Rh.* 'Lady A. Fitzwilliam' (JWH)	**S. Gennys**	*Forsythia* 'Brilliant'
		S. Germans	*Magnolia* *mollicomata*
S. Erth	*Camellia*		
S. Ervan	previously supplied	**S. Gerrans**	Variegated Holly
		S. Giles	*Camellia* (Holman)

Virginstowe	*Rosa moyesii* (JWH) White Lilac (JWH)	**Hayle** **S. Elwyn** **Phillack** **Gwithian**	*Camellia* Judas Tree *3 Olearia macrodonta major*
S. Gluvias	4 *Davidias* (GJ) *Rosa moyesii* (JWH)	**Helston**	*Magnolia alba superba,* *Clianthus,* *Leptospermum* (DS)
Godolphin	Golden-leafed *Laburnum*		
S. Gorran	3 *Hydrangeas* 'Goliath' and 'Madame Mouillère'	**Hessenford**	*Magnolia* x *soulangeana* 'Alexandrina'
S. Michael Caerhays	*Camellia* (C. Williams)	**Downderry**	to follow
Grade	2 *Olearia macrodonta maj.* 2 *Hydrangea* 'Goliath'	**S. Hilary**	*Camellia williamsii* (JWH)
		Illogan	*Prunus* 'Fugenzo' (D.Thomas)
Ruan Minor	2 *O. macrodonta major*	**I. of Scilly S. Mary**	*Phoenix canariensis* (DS)
Gulval	*Magnolia campbellii* *Clethra arborea* (DS)	**S. Issey**	*Magnolia mollicomata*
		S. Ive	*Camellia*
Gwennap	*Rh.* 'Lady A. Fitzwilliam' (JWH)	**S. Ives**	2 *Camellias* (1 from Holman)
Gwinear	*Chaenomeles*	**Jacobstow Warbstow**	*Camellia* (JWH) *Chaenomeles* 2 *Rosa moyesii* (JWH) 2 *Olearias*
Halsetown	*Camellia* (Holman)		

S. Juliot	*Camellia*
Lesnewth	*Camellia*
S. Just, Penwith	2 *Quercus ilex Senecios* etc. (AF)
S. Just, Roseland	*Magnolia mollicomata* (JWH)
Kea	*Magnolia mollicomata*
Kenwyn	*Magnolia wilsonii* (JWH)
S. Keverne	*Rh.* 'Lady A. Fitzwilliam' (JWH)
S. Kew	*Magnolia alba superba*
Kilkhampton	2 *Chaenomeles Griselinia* (JWH)
Ladock	2 Tree Myrtles (AF)
Lamorran w. **Tresillian**	*Camellia* 2 *Cupressus* 'Allumii' (Martyn)
Merther	*Drimys* (JWH) *Davidia* (GJ) *Hoheria* (DS)
S. Michael Penkivel	*Magnolia mollicomata*

Landewednack	*Camellia williamnsii* (JWH)
Landrake	*Escallonia* 'Glory of Donard'
S. Erney	*Escallonia* 'Donard Seedling'
Landulph	*Rh.* 'Lady A. Fitzwilliam' (JWH)
Laneast	*Azalea* 'Noordtiana'
Lanhydrock	*Camellia Davidia* (GJ)
Lanlivery	*Ilex maderensis*
Lanlivet	5 *Azaleas* (Martyn)
Lanner	*Chaenomeles*
Lanreath	*Camellia*
Lansallos	*Senecios, Olearias* (AF)
Lanteglos	*Camellia williamsii* (JWH)
Camelford	Wintersweet (JWH)
Lanteglos, Fowey	*Senecios Olearias* (AF)

Launcells	*Prunus longipes*	**Mabe**	*Eucryphia nymansensis*
Launceston			
S. Mary	6 *Azaleas* (Martyn)	**S. Mabyn**	2 *Arbutus*
S. Stephen	*Camellia*	**Madron**	*Camellia*
S. Thomas	Italian Cypress	**Morvah**	*Senecios, Olearias* (AF)
Lawhitton	*Camellia* 'J.C. Williams'		2 *O. macrodonta major*
Lelant	*Camellia williamsii* (JWH)	**Maker Rame**	*Chaenomeles* *Senecios, Olearias* (AF)
S. Levan	*Camellia*		
Lewannick	*Azaleas* (Martyn)	**Manaccan**	*Eucryphia nymansensis* *Magnolia campbellii* (parishioner)
Lezant	*Rh.* 'Lady Rosebury'		
Linkinhorne	*Camellia*	**S. Anthony**	*Embothrium longifolium*
Liskeard	2 *Camellias* 7 *Azaleas* (Martyn)	**Marazion**	*Camellia*
		Marhamchurch	*Chaenomeles*
Looe	*Cornus capitata* (JWH)	**S. Martin, Looe**	Judas Tree
		Mawgan	*Cytisus proliferus* (JWH)
Lostwithiel	*Camellia* *Drimys* (JWH)		*Davidia* (GJ)
		S. Martin in Meneage	*Drimys* (JWH) *Davidia* (GJ)
Ludgvan	*Camellia* (AF)		
Luxulyan	*Berberis lologensis* 'Highdown variegated'	**Mawnan**	*Viburnum betulifolius* (JWH)

S. Mellion	*Magnolia sieboldii*	**Mylor**	*Eucalyptus coccifera* (JWH)
Pillaton	to follow		
		S. Neot	*Azalea* 'Mrs A. Wery'
Menheniot	*Camellia* (Holman)		
		S. Newlyn E.	Chaenomeles
S. Merryn	2 *Chaenomeles* 3 *Olearias*	**Newlyn**	*Camellia*
Mevagissey	*Camellia* 2 *Azaleas* (Martyn)	**Newquay**	4 *Olearia macrodonta major*
S. Mewan	*Camellia williamsii* (JWH)	**North Hill**	2 *Arbutus*
		N. Petherwin	4 *Azaleas* (Martyn)
Millbrook	*Hamamelis mollis Mahonia japonica*		
		N. Tamerton	*Camellia* 'J.C. Williams'
S. Minver	*Camellia*		
S. Enodoc	3 Sea Buckthorn *Olearias, Senecios* (AF)	**Padstow**	*Crinodendron*
S. Michael	*Buddleia*	**Par**	*Rh.* 'Lady A. Fitzwilliam' (JWH)
Rock	'Royal Red'		
Mithian	3 *Hydrangeas*		
		Paul	*Camellia* 'Preston Rose'
Morval	*Cornus capitata* (JWH)		
		Pelynt	*Camellia* 'E. Rothschild'
Morwenstow	*Chaenomeles Senecios, Olearias* (AF)		
		Pendeen	*Camellia* Tree Myrtle, *Olearias* (AF)
Mt. Hawke	*Camellia*		
Mullion	*Metrosideros robusta*		

Penponds	*Prunus* 'Tai Haku' (D. Thomas)	**Quethiock**	2 *Rosa moyesii* (JWH)
Penwerris	*Camellias*	**Redruth**	*Rh.* 'Lady A. Fitzwilliam' (JWH)
Penzance			
S. John	*Magnolia alba superba*	**Roche**	*C.* 'Adolphe Audusson'
S. Mary	*Camellia williamsii* (JWH)	**Ruan**	*Hamamelis*
S. Paul	*Camellia*	**Lanihorne**	*mollis*
		Philleigh	*Forsythia* 'Lynwood'
Perranuthnoe	*Camellia* (Holman)		
		Saltash	*Magnolia alba superba*
Perranzabuloe	*Chaenomeles*		
Perranporth	*Berberis darwinii* 'Flame' *Berberis stenophylla coccinea*	**S. Sampson**	*Camellia* 'Elizabeth Rothschild'
		Sancreed	*Camellia*
S. Petroc Minor	*Camellia*	**Sennen**	*Olearias, Senecios* (AF)
Porthleven	*Cedrus atlantica glauca*	**Sheviock**	*Prunus subhirtella autumnalis rosea*
Port Isaac	*Olearias, Senecios* (AF)	**Sithney**	*Chaenomeles*
Poughill	*Camellia*	**South Hill**	2 *Azaleas* (Martyn) *Hoheria* (DS)
Poundstock	*Camellia williamsii* (JWH)	**Callington**	2 *Azaleas* (Martyn) *Davidia* (GJ) *Drimys* (JWH)
Probus	*Camellia* (Holman)		

S. Petherwin	*Camellia* 'White Swan'	**Torpoint**	*Rh.* 'Lady A. Fitzwilliam' (JWH)
S. Stephen Brannel	*Camellia* (Holman) 2 *Cupressus* 'Allumii' (Martyn)	**Tregony**	*Magnolia mollicomata*
		Treleigh	*Prunus* 'Fugenzo' (D. Thomas)
S. Stephen Saltash	2 *Quercus Ilex*	**Tresmere Treneglos**	*Forsythia* to follow
Stoke Climsland	Camellia 5 *Azaleas* (Martyn)	**Tremaine** **Tresco**	to follow *Phoenix canariensis* (DS)
Stratton	*Prunus* 'Fugenzo' (D. Thomas)	**Treslothan**	*Camellia* (Holman)
S. Stythians Perran- ar-worthal	*Camellia* *Viburnum betulifolium* (JWH)	**Treverbyn** **Truro**	*Camellia*
Talland	*Camellia* 'Juno'	**S. George**	*Camellia* (Holman)
S. Teath Michaelstow	*Prunus incisa* Camellia (Maj. Muir)	**S. Mary** **S. John**	*Camellia* 2 *Azaleas* (Martyn) *Magnolia globosa* (JWH)
Delabole	12 *Olearias* *Senecios* (AF)	**S. Paul**	*Berberis lologensis* 2 *B. wilsonae* (JWH)
Tideford	*Camellia*	**Tuckingmill**	*Camellia*
Tintagel	*Chaenomeles* 'Rowallane' *Olearias, Senecios* (AF) 3 *Olearias*	**S. Tudy**	*Camellia* (Mrs Magor)

Tywardreath	*Rh.* 'Lady A. Fitzwilliam' (JWH)	**Werrington**	*Pieris formosa* (A.M. Williams)
		Whitstone	no reply
Veryan	*Camellia* 'St Ewe' (C.Williams)	**S. Winnow**	not wanted
		S. Nectan	not wanted
Warleggan	*Chaenomeles*	**S. Veep**	not wanted
Week S. Mary	*Camellia* (Holman)	**Withiel**	*Camellia*
Wendron	*Camellia williamsii* (JWH)	**Zennor**	*Camellia*
		Towednack	*Berberis darwinii* 'Flame'
S. Wenn	*Camellia* 'Juno' (JWH)